Celebrating the Egyptian Gods

Celebrating the Egyptian Gods

by Sharon LaBorde

A Golden Age Publication

Celebrating the Egyptian Gods

Copyright 2018 Sharon LaBorde. All rights reserved.

A Golden Age Publication. Printed by Lulu Press.

ISBN: 978-1-387-91917-8

All rights reserved. This book, or parts thereof, may not be reproduced in any form without written permission except by a reviewer who may quote brief passages in review, or by individual users posting online video blogs.

First Edition, 2018

Acknowledgments

No great undertaking reaches completion alone. For this work, I owe deep thanks for the input of fellow Kemetics about their practice, including (but not limited to): Amanda, Drew, Linda, Lotus, Nathaniel, Mary and Peter, Rin, Romeo, Sah, Sean, Yamanu, and Zabora. All of the people who participate in the Kemetic Reform group have been supportive with their enthusiasm and encouragement, as have my wonderful YouTube viewers over these years.
I could not do this without all of you!

And especially, most importantly,
to my husband and most stalwart
supporter. Daryn, I love you always.

Contents

I. Introduction	**11**
II. Working With Deities	**15**
Requesting Dream Oracles	17
Meditation	19
Offering Rituals	24
Iru and Its Symbolism	26
Sources and Pronunciation Guide	35
III. The Notjeru	
The Great Ennead - Major Deities	**41**
Amun	41
Anubis	46
Atum	48
Bast	49
Bes	52
Djehuty	54
Geb	57
Hathor	59
Horus	63
Isis	67
Khopri	72
Khnum	72
Khonsu	75
Ma'at	78
Min	80
Mut	83
Neith	86
Nephthys	91
Nut	93
Osiris	96

Ptah	**102**
Ra	**105**
Sakhmet	**112**
Serket	**116**
Seshat	**118**
Seth	**120**
Shu	**123**
Sobek	**126**
Sokar	**129**
Tawret	**131**
Tefnut	**133**
Wadjit	**135**
Wepwawet	**138**
The Little Ennead - Lesser-Known Deities	**141**
Aker	**143**
Ammut	
Anuket	
Aton	**144**
Duamutef	**145**
Hapy	
Hat-Mehyt	**146**
Heka	
Heqat	**147**
Hu	
Ihy	**148**
Imsety	
Inhur	
Maahes	**149**
Mafdet	
Meretseger	**150**
Montu	
Nefertum	**11**

Nehmetawai
Nekhebet
Nun — 152
Pakhet
Qebehsenuef — 153
Ra'et-Tawy
Rennutet — 154
Satit
Ta'it — 155
Tatenen
Tutu — 156
Wennut — 157

The Nubian Ennead — 158
  Amesemi — 158
  Apademak — 159
  Aqedise
  Arensnuphis
  Mandulis — 160
  Sebiumeker

IV. A Calendar of Feast Days — 161
  Understanding the Egyptian Liturgical Year — 161
  Observances Then and Now — 166
  The Calendar — 169
  Special Readings for Feast Days — 186

V. Online Resources — 197

VI. Bibliography — 200

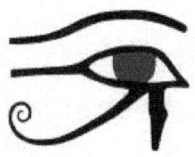

Introduction

Iiu em hotep!

This phrase means "Come in peace" in the ancient Egyptian, or *Kemetic*, language. Today Kemetic Pagans use it as a formal greeting, a way of saying "Welcome," most often to a new online forum or social media group. But perhaps, if you're familiar with Paganism through online videos, you might recognize another greeting drawn from colloquial ancient Egyptian. So, *Nyny!* Hello, and welcome to a different sort of 'Kemetic How-to Guide'.

Over the eight years (and counting) that I've been producing *The Kemetic How-to Guide* on YouTube, my most common viewer questions have centered around the Egyptian Gods and Goddesses: requesting information about a specific deity, what offerings They like most, or how best to work with those deities in personal practice. Answering these questions presents new challenges that I always meet with enthusiasm, for two reasons. The first comes in the form of humorous props, visual aids and video clips that allow me to drag unlikely pop culture references into a discussion of ancient Egyptian Gods. I find the combination of video editing, comedy and education in making those videos absolutely irresistible.

The second, closely related reason has also served as the catalyst for this book. By answering practical questions about the Egyptian Gods, I can speak of Them in the present tense. The Gods, in turn, can step out of dry academic theories about a world so far removed in time from our own and emerge with vivid relevance into our own lives. Egyptologists are trained to view religion with detached skepticism, which is the necessary price of unbiased scientific inquiry. But for me, to speak of worshiping Egyptian Gods and Goddesses *now*, in the twenty-first century, is to speak of active faith. In my videos, I share stories of my personal experiences with Them, and often I read with delight and amazement the responses of fellow Pagans who have experienced the same Gods and Goddesses.

In my first book, *Following the Sun: A Practical Guide to Egyptian Religion*, I concentrated on describing major Egyptian deities using what we know from ancient sources, citing current academic works. Egyptologists on the whole may never appreciate the 'lived experience' of religion, (although that may change - see *Profane Egyptologists: The Modern Revival of Ancient Egyptian Religion* by Paul Harrison), but their work still provides us as Pagans with an absolutely invaluable source of material. I continue to draw from their scholarship even now. Here, however, I can also describe the Gods as I and other Pagans know Them today. I can address other frequent questions such as, "Who is the Patron(ess) of (*insert concept here*)?" or, surely the most directly personal query, "Who should I pray to about such-and-such problem?"

In answering those questions, however, I can also more fully expound certain ideas not well-suited to video. In ten or fifteen minutes of airtime I can cover a range of trivia about a particular deity; but in the process I might lead viewers to conclude, incorrectly, that said deity *only* relates to those topics covered. This mis-conclusion actually represents the overriding tendency in modern thinking towards polytheism: to handle X concern, you must ask X god. I liken this mode of thinking to playing a game of *Pokémon*. "Oh no, my dog just swallowed a bug! Anubis, I choose *you!*" Perhaps this 'Pokémon polytheism' derives from our society's Roman origins, where abstract concepts routinely became divinized and Imperial priests sacrificed to the gods of enemy countries in order to gain victory over their armies in battle. But such compartmentalized thinking does disservice to Egyptian religion. Common human concerns such as healing sickness or finding love could have multiple Egyptian deities presiding over them; for healing, would you prefer to invoke Sakhmet, Isis (Aset), Serket, or Thoth (Djehuty)? You could ask Hathor for help in matters of love - or Isis, or even Ptah, as did a young scribe in an ancient song about the city of Memphis. Thus we have the dilemma faced by many newcomers to polytheism: with so many options, how does one choose their own personal deities?

By offering both historical and modern information about individual deities, I hope to make those choices a little easier. In the next section, I also explain more about 'working with' deities and what that phrase entails, so that readers can learn and implement new spiritual tools for themselves. Empowering fellow Pagans to explore the Egyptian pantheon and discover their own patron Gods and Goddesses is also critical to avoid yet another pitfall related to 'Pokémon polytheism', one that I call 'personality test polytheism'.

Chances are, you've already encountered actual 'What Egyptian God Are You?' quizzes (and ones for other pantheons) on social media, most of them rather inane and goofy in their construction. But some Pagans seem to seriously interpret polytheism in much the same way as these quizzes. Certain Kemetic traditions in particular seem afflicted with a chronic case of 'personality test polytheism', and conflate the attributes of a particular deity with the personality traits of that deity's devotees. Thus, followers of Set are expected to be upstarts, devotees of Isis (or Aset) supposedly act haughty toward others, meanwhile having a morbid sense of humor indicates the patronage of Anubis.

But just as the Egyptian Gods, or *Notjeru*, are too multifaceted to be pigeonholed into specific roles like so many Pokémon characters, so too are Their relationships with Their followers. Personal traits or affinity may suggest the patronage of a particular God or Goddess, but another deity with an opposite personality may play an equally important role in someone's life as a teacher, guardian or even catalyst. Quite often, Pagans report that the relationships they have with particular deities change over time; this is normal. As we grow and change, the presences of some deities in our lives waxes and wanes. This reflects badly on neither ourselves or the Notjeru; Their plans are simply greater than we can discern at a given moment.

In describing the Notjeru, I also cover another aspect of patronage that sees too seldom mention elsewhere: modern professions. If the Egyptian Gods are aware of our lives, They must also by extension be aware of the modern world we inhabit. 'Living religions' grow and adapt to new needs, hence the folk saint Santa Muerte's patronage extends to sex workers (many of them transgendered) in Mexico, while Joan of Arc has become the patron saint of women in the military. Why would the Notjeru not adapt as well?

Finally, while this book is written primarily for Egyptian Pagans, I try to avoid deep jargon or obscure 'Pagan' references wherever possible, so that anyone wishing to gain a deeper understanding of Egyptian religion can enjoy it. As our society gradually grows more aware of its plurality, sensitive minds might wish to learn more about the chosen deity of a friend, colleague or family member. I offer this work a resource for those supporters as well.

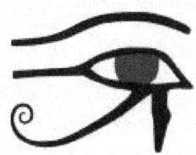

Working With Deities

What does it mean to "work with" a deity? Read through online discussions or comments and that phrase comes up with regularity. Some Pagans mean 'spell work' when they talk about 'working' with a deity, but I would admonish beginners to consider magick and spell casting, or *Heka* in Kemetic traditions, as a secondary aspect of 'working with' the Notjeru. Much of Egyptian magick is not suitable beginner's material. *Heka* involves energy, effort and research. To explain by example, would you rather tackle an important group project with someone you've only just met; or with someone you know, who knows you, and with whose style you're already familiar? Working *heka* is basically a spiritual joint project between you as the practitioner and the Gods that you invoke, so it's more likely to bear results if you already have a rapport with your partners.

That example actually brings us to a better definition of 'working with' a God or Goddess. Put simply, it involves getting to know Them and learning how to listen to Them. Different Notjeru 'speak' to us in different ways, and They may not even speak the same way to all of Their devotees. Learning to work with a God or Goddess means figuring out how you personally connect with Them.

Chances are that, if you're reading this with a specific deity in mind, you've already had an initial encounter with Them. Many people recount having dreams, sometimes quite vivid, about a God or Goddess - or perhaps one of Their symbols.

Totem animals and associations for specific deities will be addressed under Their individual entries. Still other Pagans encounter an Egyptian God or Goddess during an eclectic Wiccan ritual or a divination session, and set out to learn more about Them afterward.

That said, however, I must address one practice used in various Pagan and Kemetic traditions which, in my experience, has the potential to be dangerously misleading. Wiccans call it 'Drawing Down the Sun' or 'Drawing Down the Moon'; eclectic Pagans have variously called it 'aspecting' or 'channeling'; and the Kemetic Orthodox calls their own version '*s'aq*', commonly pronounced 'sack' or 'sock'. All of these names describe the phenomenon of having a God or Goddess speak through an individual, temporarily inhabiting that person's body and interacting with others through it.

Skeptics, of course, would question whether or not channeling a deity is even possible. I can relate that I have seen both brief, but genuine, instances and hackneyed, overhyped attempts. Never assume that someone claiming the ability to channel (or *s'aq*) a deity has legitimacy based solely on their reputation; I felt the Mother Goddess more clearly in the embrace of a humble Wiccan priestess from a rural coven than I did from an Indian guru celebrated around the world as the "Hugging Saint". Nor is the ability to effectively channel spiritual entities commonly found, either. Temporarily allowing another spirit into one's own body does not come easily, and most of us are too firmly attached within our own bodies to allow it (and for good reason!). I have known someone for many years who has that ability, but their skill comes at the price of passing out more easily, and having nearly left their physical form permanently on several occasions.

Another complication comes from the sheer disparity in scale, spiritually speaking, between a human being and a God. Humans can channel other humans (as 'spirit mediums' do) far more easily; and character actors channel fictional entities all the time as part of their job. But Gods and Goddess are so much older, so much more vast in Their power and experience, and yet at the same time so unfamiliar with the limitations of a flesh-and-blood body, that much of Their essence is either lost or garbled in 'translation' when They are being channeled. Even when someone with genuine ability does the channeling, some of their own personal traits can seep through the deity's words - but a less accomplished hack will simply relate their own words and ideas as those of the God's. Sadly, some people accept these fraudulent 'messages' as legitimate.

With this in mind, I strongly advocate that anyone seeking a relationship with an Egyptian God or Goddess (or a deity from any pantheon, for that matter) learn how to listen and encounter the Divine for themselves. Do not depend on the words and claims of some supposed mouthpiece for the Gods! Even if they relate some scrap of information that appears relevant, you still miss the fuller experience of approaching your Gods personally, one-on-one, with no one acting as a middleman or -woman.

So how does someone actually begin working with a deity? If you're reading this book, you've already taken the first step: *learning*. The more you educate yourself about a particular God or Goddess, the more readily you will be able to recognize Their signs. The appearance of a bird or animal, occurrence of a natural (or unnatural) phenomenon, dream imagery, or even certain fragrances could all act as heralds of a deity's presence. By familiarizing yourself with an Egyptian deity's historical attributes, you also give yourself the benefit of work already done by worshipers in ancient times. Modern Paganism continues to take the worship of the Notjeru in new directions, but the religion of ancient Egypt remains our common heritage and our starting point.

Requesting Dream Oracles

Sometimes beginners, unsure of where to go next, grow anxious looking for signs from the Notjeru. First, a word of advice: *relax*. Take your time, read, learn, and enjoy the journey. But if you feel the need to ask for messages via dreams, you can try taking some cues from a corpus of work known as the Greek Magical Papyri. A collection of spells and divination manuals written in Greek and Coptic that span the last centuries of antiquity, many of their prescribed methods would make modern Craft users blanch in shock. However, certain common elements occur repeatedly in the entries requesting dream oracles, without the need for sacrificial animals or bizarre ingredients. Put in a modern context, here are the most basic steps:

1. Purify yourself. Take a shower, or a scented bath if you prefer. This gives you an opportunity to not only cleanse your body, but also clear your thoughts and center yourself.

2. Light a pure white candle. In ancient times, oil lamps were not just ritual tools, but the primary means of illumination after dark. So when dream manuals called for a user to extinguish their lamp - always one made of clay that was not red, because of negative associations with the color - it was time to go to bed. Here, you can light a white candle (again, to avoid any specific color associations and to symbolize purity) in your bedroom or at your altar space.

3. Say a prayer to the candle. This prayer doesn't have to be elaborate, but you'll want to be specific in your requests. It could be something as simple as, "Oh light of goodness and truth, show me Who is to be my guide, answer me in truth this night." Spend as much time as you need in prayer or reflection, but try to keep your thoughts calm and peaceful. You're taking a positive step forward in your own spiritual journey; treat it as such. Also, while this should go without saying...

4. Don't talk to anyone before bed. Ancient spell authors make this point repeatedly - they could never have imagined a world with the Internet! Put away that smart phone before you begin your purification. Modern studies have repeatedly warned of the stress- and insomnia-inducing effects of checking email or social media before bed, and that's without considering the effects it might have on spiritual work and one's dream state. If you share a house with family or roommates, it might be harder to avoid talking to them before going to bed. Don't be uncivil toward anyone, but you could try explaining beforehand that you want to try some relaxation techniques before bed and you don't plan on being conversational.

5. Extinguish your candle and go to sleep. Make sure you've given yourself enough hours of sleep to allow for dreaming - three or four won't be enough for your body to go through the necessary cycles to reach REM (Rapid Eye Movement) sleep, which is where most dreams occur. According to the American Sleep Association, we optimally spend two hours out of each night dreaming. For our purposes, that means two hours' worth of potential contact with the spiritual world.

You may also want to try keeping a dream journal. (This was even suggested in a creative writing class I took once.) To better document your dreams, keep your journal in your bedroom where you can write down what you remember soon after getting up. If you have to recall your dreams later in the day, try laying in your favorite sleeping position to jog your memory - though, if you're tired, this may lead you to more dreams to write about later! Dream journaling could be particularly useful for spotting recurring themes or patterns over time, especially if nothing obvious comes up in one or two nights. If you're plagued with frequent or recurring nightmares, try reducing stress in your life wherever you can and, if that doesn't help, seek a professional counselor. Tackling other problems in our lives still counts toward our spiritual journey.

Meditation

Many of the world's religious traditions claim some form of meditation, and even secular Western society has come to extol the virtues of meditation for stress relief and holistic medicine. Much of what we commonly know of as 'meditation', though, might be better described as 'contemplation' or 'reflection': placing ourselves in a serene environment where we can ponder spiritual matters, introspect, and hopefully gain some insight in the process.

That is not the type of meditation I will be describing here. *Meditation* as understood in Eastern traditions, especially in (but not limited to) Buddhism, has as its purpose the honing of one's concentration, reaching altered - but not reduced - states of consciousness, and heightening spiritual awareness. While our goal is not quite the same as Buddhist enlightenment, we can still learn several highly effective techniques from their repertoire. In the physical world, we listen with our ears; in order to listen to the spiritual world, we must use our minds. Bombarded as we are in today's constant-stimulation ethos, developing the ability to concentrate and direct our awareness is essential to developing our minds, our 'spiritual ears', so to speak.

Silent seated meditation is the form best known in the West, but a meditative state can be accomplished in many different ways. Repetitious, monotonous activities can also create an altered state of consciousness. The famous Zen gardens of Japan look so beautiful not simply because of their austerely balanced designs, for example, but also because the Zen monks themselves use the otherwise tedious tasks of raking patterns in sand, picking up stray leaves and tending the temple grounds as a form of repetitive meditation. Coming back to Egypt, the whirling dervishes of Sufi traditions use their spinning dances and dhikr chants to achieve an altered state of consciousness which they describe as a 'union with God'.

That said, seated meditation does offer the most accessible method for a beginner. Once you gain some proficiency in the basics of concentration, you can begin experimenting with visualizations, chanting, or other techniques. To get started, let's consider the physical, then the mental aspects of this practice.

Physical aspects: Start by picking a quiet, comfortable place where you are least likely to be disturbed. If your bedroom is the most private space available, don't use your bed - you're more likely to either fall asleep, or potentially disrupt your sleep patterns later by associating your bed with something besides sleeping. If you have an altar space already, that presents an ideal space in which to incorporate meditation practice.

However you choose to sit, make sure you're comfortable. Sit up straight, but not too rigid, and try to maintain a good posture. For many Buddhist traditions, the ideal pose is 'full lotus', where your legs are crossed and each of your feet rest on top of the opposite thigh - but that same pose would have at least one of my chiropractors screaming in protest, hence my advice to *sit in a manner that will not cause pain*. Our aim is to improve our lives, not make them worse. Rest your hands in your lap, and try not to close your eyes completely. Find something upon which to rest your gaze - a candle, statue or object on your altar can serve as a useful focus point. Whatever you use, avoid staring at something with which you already have strong mental associations, or that will draw you into a train of thought as you gaze upon it. This brings us to our next set of considerations.

Mental aspects: Inevitably as you sit down to meditate, you will notice your mind wandering - if not running around like a caffeine-jacked Chihuahua. "Did I put the butter back in the fridge? Ooh, I better check that message once I'm done here. Are we still on with so-and-so for this weekend?" And on and on the bullet train of thought goes...unless we tell our brains to sit still and be quiet for a few minutes. But how do we do that?

You can simply 'try not to think', meaning to not verbalize any thoughts in your mind at all, for as long as possible; but this technique is highly difficult. If you've never tried to do it before, it can feel much like holding your breath. Instead, a better method for beginners involves concentrating on that simple act of breathing. As you sit relaxed, draw in a slow, steady breath through your nose; feel your chest expand as it fill your lungs; then release it, steadily and completely. Concentrate on nothing but this breathing exercise. Let it develop a rhythm. Some meditation manuals (along with Mr. Miyagi in *Karate Kid II*) prescribe that you breathe in through your nose and out through your mouth, but in my own experience that can sometimes serve as its own distraction. Do it that way only if it feels natural to you. The overall objective of this breathing exercise is to stop your mind from wandering uncontrollably, to put the figurative brakes on your train of thought, if only for a short while.

Next you can try picking a focal point somewhere in your meditation space and simply observe it. Don't verbalize any observations about this object in your mind, such as its name, size, color, and so forth. It may help to remind yourself that these are only qualifiers we place on external objects in the first place; to paraphrase a Zen koan, 'flowers are unaware that they are fragrant and garbage does not know its own smell'. Concentrate on your focal point, block out the rest of the world, and simply 'be' along with your object of focus.

The reason why we are trying to temporarily halt our brains' tendencies to analyze and verbalize is because our thoughts represent the 'speech' of our minds. If we are constantly talking, how can we hear anyone else speak? (Some people seem unable to do this in physical terms, let alone mentally.) When the Gods speak, we will hear it in our minds as words, pictures, or even sudden memories that seem to 'come out of nowhere'.

Once you get a feel for this state of concentration, you can try introducing meditative aids such as music or chanting. I recommend using music that either has no words, or else has words in a language you do not speak, so you don't find yourself thinking about the lyrics. You can use any genre that agrees with you; I've been able to concentrate using everything from trance techno to traditional Muslim dhikr chants. If you use a chant or mantra in English (or your birth language, if it's different), keep it short and sweet. Make it something that can be repeated rhythmically and fluidly. One good example from the book *Circle of Isis* is "X, Lord/Lady, teach me of Thee." (So, by way of example, "Anubis, Lord, teach me of Thee," or "Hathor, Lady, teach me of Thee".) As you recite your mantra, build a steady rhythm - not too fast - until you lose awareness of the words. Eventually the words will just become sounds that you no longer hear, and instead the God or Goddess you invoke will speak.

A final strategy involves chanting in a foreign language, often in archaic form. This method takes practice and memorization, but it can be done; Nichiren Buddhists chant sutras in Sino-Japanese as part of their daily rituals. For those intrepid enough to tackle this technique, I am including Egyptian-language hymns and addresses to as many Notjeru as possible within Their individual entries, plus a pronunciation guide at the end of this chapter. With a little persistence - and concentration - it can make for a wonderful devotional meditation.

After Meditation: The types of meditation I've just described can create powerful altered states of consciousness. But use them wisely. If you experience agitation, headaches or other noticeable side effects while trying to meditate, stop and consult a doctor or counselor. A small percentage of people actually experience a condition called relaxation-induced anxiety (RIA), and just trying to 'tough it out' won't help.

If you aren't planning on going to bed soon after meditation, then give yourself at least an hour's time to get back to your regular level of mental activity. Avoid reading, listening to podcasts or watching YouTube video blogs during that hour, or doing anything else that requires critical thinking or emotional involvement. Deep meditation works in the opposite direction because it allows your mind to be more receptive and less analytical. In religious or personal practice, this is a beautiful experience; but when other human beings are involved, it weakens your resistance to outside suggestion. (An entirely new field of study is finding that long hours of continuous Internet activity can have that same effect - a note of caution for gamers, those who still IRC chat, and heavy social media users.) My whole purpose in explaining meditation practices is to offer you a tool that you can use on your own terms, without handing someone else control over your own mental and spiritual development. The world has enough schemes and religions that do this already.

Regardless of which meditation techniques you use, be patient with your progress and don't give up. Learning how to meditate and build awareness represent a lifelong process of growth. It is not something you can master in 'a year and a day'. But it can add a tremendous depth to your spiritual practice, regardless of where your path ultimately takes you.

Offering Rituals

A newcomer to Paganism whose only prior religious background comes from Abrahamic monotheism (Judaism, Christianity and Islam) might find the concept of ritually offering food, beverages, incense and material items to deities to be strange or even simplistic. Even highly educated Egyptologists who recorded temple texts in person and published translations of them often described these ancient offering rites in rather condescending terms. Serge Sauneron writes in *The Priests of Ancient Egypt* (via English translation by David Lorton):

> To be sure, in many ways it seems purely material, and the notion of a deity who is washed, dressed, and fed does not result in a very spiritual picture of the ritual.

To Dr. Sauneron's credit, he does go on to say that "conclusions regarding the Egyptian ritual based solely on these...impressions would surely be unfair." But this sort of scholarly looking-down-the-nose at ancient religious practices presents a major stumbling block for Pagans who seek Egyptological sources in order to understand Egyptian religion; these publications can tell us the *what* and *how* about offering rites, but fail to give satisfactory answers on *why* offering rituals were so important. Too often their explanations seem to suggest that the entire ancient Egyptian religious establishment was neurotically fixated on "[i]solation, purity of the temple and its officiants, absolute rigor in the performance of the rituals, [and] punctuality of the offerings" lest the entire structure of the known world fail (our quote again coming from Sauneron). Could the Egyptian religion have really been that inflexible?

The worst part comes when some Kemetic Pagans, either Independent or belonging to a specific tradition, insist that modern practice follow this exact same slavish interpretation of ancient Egyptian practices in the name of 'historical accuracy'. Don't dare consecrate an altar statue, they warn, unless you are prepared to make offerings to it *every day*. The Gods will go hungry and become upset if you don't! And don't offer modern candies or other items to a deity, that's inappropriate. (Years ago on the forum eCauldron, a follower of Bast posted that she had offered a stuffed animal that she felt Bast had specifically asked for; purists on the forum actually trolled her for making an 'improper' offering.) Attitudes that began as scholarly ham-handedness about an ancient polytheistic faith become tools for ridicule and control in the hands of unscrupulous Kemetics. The most telling example comes from the introductory guide for the Kemetic Orthodox, which warns newcomers to stop performing any ritual practices they had been using previously, until they learn how to correctly perform the Kemetic Orthodox rite of 'Senut' (which is itself contingent upon a number of strict purity and altar guidelines interpreted from ancient temple records).

How you begin your own Pagan practice, including offerings and other rituals, is no one else's business. Let me re-iterate: *Let no one frighten you away from praying and offering to your chosen Gods as you see fit.* As you learn to listen to your Gods, They will tell you what gifts or behaviors They do and do not prefer. You may well find through further research that your instincts are confirmed by ancient sources. But sometimes you may discover that a God or Goddess has developed a new affinity, or permits certain actions that do not match historical record. In these cases, remember that They grow and evolve, too. To give just one example, chickens were unknown to Egypt before the New Kingdom era; but by Greco-Roman times, an unblemished rooster became a staple offering to invoke solar deities such as Ra, and He even took on a rooster avatar in the so-called 'Abrasax gems'. Why should His ability to adopt new favored offerings or attributes have stopped in Roman times?

Iru and Its Symbolism

I have already given two variations of an offering ritual, in both short and long form, in *Following the Sun* and *Circle of the Sun*. You can also watch one being performed in my YouTube video, *Kemetic How-to Guide: A Basic Ritual*. But here I can further break down the components of the *Iru* rite (coming from the Egyptian word for "things done") and explain in greater detail the meanings - the *why* that underlies the *what* - behind each step of the ritual. Then you can more fully appreciate and use the (slightly expanded) *Iru* ritual that follows. Let's look at each element:

Lighting a candle - For the ancient Egyptians, the flame from a torch, oil lamp or candle repeated the sun's power in miniature. At night or in the deep recesses of hidden chambers, a lit lamp pushed back against the darkness, creating a zone of safety and order. For these reasons a ritual lamp was equated, through statements recited as it was being lit, with the Eye of Horus (*Udjat*-eye). The word *udjat* meant "sound" or "healthy", and it signified the eye that Horus lost while battling Set to avenge his father. His eye was restored to him afterward, taking on powerful properties of healing, protection and completion that are regularly invoked in Egyptian rituals.

In celestial terms, the Eye of Horus can represent the moon, which wanes (is injured), disappears, then waxes (heals) again. But as an ancient god of the sky, Horus' two eyes could also represent both the sun and moon. Further, by the Late Period the Eye of Horus became conflated with the Eye of Ra, which signified solar goddesses such as Sakhmet, Bast, Tefnut, Hathor and others. Hence, this powerful symbol of healing and order can itself take on solar meanings. When invoked in the candle-lighting part of a ritual, the Eye of Horus is welcomed as if it were the sun rising at dawn, casting out evil and clearing the way for the Gods.

Playing a sistrum - While they are not crucial for observing a ritual, using a sistrum adds wonderful dimensions of sound and symbolism to its performance. The ancients compared the shaking of sistra (plural of 'sistrum') to shaking bunches of papyrus stalks in the river marshes. Having shaken several sistrums as well as stalks of my own papyrus plant, I'm personally unsure of the sonic resemblance - perhaps the flat metal jingles in ancient sistra didn't have the same resonance that modern ones do. But more to the point, jingling sistra chased away evil. It is no coincidence that sistra were held sacred to Hathor; as an Eye of Ra goddess, She hunted down and destroyed the wicked foes of Ra. Sistra and their jingling sounds were also offered to Eye of Ra goddesses to dispel Their anger and bring about Their happiness.

Handmade sistra (and apparently even a few cast-resin ones) can be found online from time to time. You can also make one using directions from *Following the Sun*. If you can acquire or make one for yourself, using it at points indicated in ritual actually does more than give the ritual a lively punctuation, cast out negativity and call forth the Gods in joy - all very powerful reasons in their own right. Sistra are also the most emblematic ritual instruments of ancient Egypt. The Coptic and Ethiopian Orthodox churches still use smaller versions today, but sistra were first sounded in honor of the Notjeru. They have not forgotten this.

Invocation - In ancient temples, the morning service began at dawn with a litany that repeated, "Awaken in peace," to call forth the Gods from Their nocturnal rest. Modern offering rites might be performed at any time of day - thanks to livestreaming technology, I've led rituals that took place simultaneously during late afternoon for some participants and after midnight for others. But regardless of the hour, an invocation still performs the same function of inviting and welcoming the God or Goddess to join the ritual and receive Their offerings. Their arrival is likened to the sun's emergence upon the eastern horizon, or *Akhet*.

Physical offerings:

Water offering - Cool water represents refreshment and purity across cultures. In Egyptian liturgy, cool water is also identified with the Inundation - the Nile's annual flood - because of its life-giving qualities. The annual Inundation renewed the fields and brought the Egyptian landscape back to a state similar to the primeval flood, the *Nun*, that existed prior to Creation. To identify a water offering with the Inundation imbued it with properties of renewal. Further equating it to the Eye of Horus doubled its restorative effect.

Milk - Offering milk symbolizes nourishing life force, purity, and in certain contexts, rebirth. Mother goddesses frequently received milk offerings; the goddess Isis was offered milk on the festival of Her birthday. As an agent of rebirth, milk was offered to Osiris at His shrine in the temple of Isis at Philae. Milk was identified with Mehet-Uret, the 'Great Flood', a form of primeval mother goddess pictured as a cow. The Creatrix goddess Neith was especially connected to Mehet-Uret.

Incense - One of the general words for 'incense' in the ancient Egyptian language was *senotjer*, which means 'to make divine'. Incense symbolizes purity and holiness. Many of the resin ingredients used to make incense were identified as substances exuded by the Gods, such as the tears of Ra or Horus. No surprise, then, that burning incense was identified with the Eye of Horus as a cleansing, sanctifying agent.

Food offerings - A variety of foodstuffs were offered in ancient times, many of them carrying specific meanings. Cooked meat represented the hearts (or bodies) of the Gods' defeated enemies, thus ensuring cosmic order. Different fruits or vegetables could be associated with different deities, and also with fertility or renewal. Bread was a staple of life for ancient Egyptians, thus a staple offering on Egyptian altars. In fact, the hieroglyph for *hotep*, the word meaning both 'offering' and 'peace' or 'contentment', pictured a conical loaf of bread placed on a reed mat. By stating, "take this, Your bread...lift it to Your face and be at peace (*hotep*) with it", the ancients were indulging in a sacred pun. Now you, too, can appreciate their wordplay.

Although not listed specifically below, you can also offer flowers. Those symbolized rejuvenation and bounty, and were offered to the blessed dead at certain lunar and annual feasts. Beer or wine were offered to certain deities to symbolize the fructifying Inundation, the Eye of Horus, or in certain cases, appeasement of the raging Eye of Ra.

Hymns and prayers - Here is where you will "customize" the ritual to honor your chosen deity. You can read prayers you've written yourself, or choose one from the entry on that particular God or Goddess in the next chapter. If you want to meditate with your Notjer, this would be a perfect opportunity to do so. Make this part of the ritual as long or as short as you need.

Closing invocation - You've shared a meal with your Gods and spent time with Them; as a good host, now you need to give Them a polite segue so that They can take Their leave. This closing address continues the solar theme by wishing the Gods joyful passage in the Mandjet, which is Ra's solar boat that travels the daytime sky, and restful passage in Ra's nocturnal Sektet boat that traverses the Underworld.

Extinguishing the candle - Your ritual candle was identified with the Eye of Horus rising at dawn when it was lit; now that the ritual is ending, it needs to 'set' in peace. The Eye of

Horus also represented the quintessential funerary offering, having first been given to Osiris. Here you offer its power to the Gods. Typically I snuff or blow out the candle right as I get to, "You consume this Eye of Horus...". As its light departs this world and the remaining smoke wafts upward, we bid it a peaceful setting in the 'mountains of Manu', the western mountains in which Ra sets every evening.

With those elements covered, we can get underway with the *Iru* ritual. I am officially giving you permission to write in your book! I've provided space for you to write in the name (or names) of the deities you choose, plus any prayers or hymns you wish to use. If you haven't chosen a specific deity to honor yet, that's quite alright - you'll get to meet many of Them in the next chapter.

The *Iru* Ritual:

Italics indicate actions to be performed. Sentences given in regular face *indicate* words to be spoken.

Preparation - *This is a religious observance, so you'll want to treat it appropriately by doing some sort of basic purification beforehand. Wash your hands, rinse out your mouth or brush your teeth, and focus your thoughts on the act of worship you're about to perform. If you perform a water lustration, you can use this prayer:*

These cool waters are upon my hands. They purify me as Tefnut purifies me.

Hail unto You, oh Notjeru! I come unto You without falsehood and without evil.

My purity is upon my hands, my purity is within my heart, and I have cast out all evil that pertained to me.

Recite four times: I am pure. ['Iu-i wab-kui', *pronounced,* "Eeyoo-i wob koo-i'.]

Lighting the Candle:

Come in peace, bright Eye of Horus, come in peace.
 Receive the light.

The Eye of Horus shines, like Ra in the twin Horizons, and evil hides in fear of it.
 Receive the light.

The Eye of Horus destroys the enemies of Ra in all of their abodes.
 Receive the light.

The Eye of Horus comes, and I am purified with it.
 Receive the light.

Invocation: *Ring your sistrum, if you have one.*

Come in peace, oh __Thoth__! Come in peace!

You arise in the *Akhet*, oh __Thoth__, spreading Your light upon the earth. Shine upon earth as You do in heaven!

Water:

Take these, Your cool waters that are the Inundation, that they may cool Your heart.

Oh __Thoth__, these waters are the Eye of Horus, that Your heart may be refreshed.

Milk:

Milk, milk, may You taste it in Your shrine. May Your heart be refreshed with it.

I bring You this milk from the Great Flood, oh __Hethert__, that You may be purified with it.

Incense: *As you light the incense, waft its smoke over your God's statue or image.*

I give You incense, I give You incense, great of purity.

Its fragrance is the Eye of Horus. Its fragrance comes to You. It cleanses You, it adorns You, it takes its place upon Your hands.

Oh __Thoth__, I give to you this Eye of Horus, its fragrance comes to You.

Food: *Place your food offering on its dish. Hold up the dish before the God's image.*

Take this, Your bread on which Gods live. This bread is the Eye of Horus, oh __Thoth__; lift it to Your face and be at peace with it.

Offering Hymns and Prayers: *Use the space below to write any special prayers you may wish to include.*

Closing Invocation: *Ring your sistrum again*

You have come in peace, Oh _Thoth_, You have come in peace.

May you go forth in peace, Oh _Thoth_, may You go forth in peace, to every place Your immortal *ka* wishes to be. May You sail in joy in the *Mandjet*-bark and rest content in the *Sektet*-bark, and may You smile upon me, Your humble servant.

Extinguishing the Candle:
This Eye of Horus has made You great. You flourish in it, You have power in it.

Oh _Thoth_, You consume this Eye of Horus and it empowers You. The Udjat sets in the Mountains of Manu, in peace.

End of Ritual

A Note About Source Materials

We Kemetic Pagans tend to get extremely picky about ancient sources for our liturgies. Rest assured that, being just as insistent about documentation (if not more so at times) as my fellows, everything I give in this book has its origins somewhere in a translated Egyptian text. My original *Iru* ritual from *Following* and *Circle of the Sun* drew from the Offering portions of the Pyramid Texts. The newer version you just read comes from the *Ritual of Amenophis I*, a daily offering ritual performed at Amunhotep I (Amenophis I)'s memorial temple in Karnak in which the deceased pharaoh was identified with Amun. Despite being used nearly a thousand years after the Pyramid Texts, its basic essence remained largely the same. Beware, however, of the tempting conclusion that some of my fellow Kemetics have put into print: ancient Egyptian liturgy did *not* remain 'static and unchanging throughout their history'. We need only compare the Cannibal Hymn from the Pyramid Texts of King Unis with the Forty-Two Declarations of Innocence from the Book of the Dead to catch a glimpse of just how far Egyptian religious thought could progress. Particularly with temple liturgies, they seemed fond of keeping basic ideas but adding new verses or elements over time, as evidenced in the *Ritual of Amenophis I*.

Ultimately, this is why I advocate editing source texts where necessary as opposed to slavishly copying them into modern rituals. When done carefully, with the original intent of the work kept in mind, the end result is neither haphazard nor blasphemous. Instead, it echoes the same meanings and even the same phrasing as the ancient work, but with a sense and presentation that modern readers can better understand and utilize.

That said, many of the hymns and prayers that follow in the next chapter draw directly from ancient sources, including the Pyramid Texts; Coffin Texts; the Book of the Dead; temple liturgies from Denderah, Edfu, Karnak, Hibis and Philae; the so-called Greek Magical Papyri, particularly the London-Leiden Papyrus; and hymns or divine titles recorded on private monuments. But because some deities have no complete surviving hymns - Bastet is but one example - interpretive work using partial sources must sometimes be done. The results will hopefully capture all the flavor and essence of the original Egyptian sources, put together in a modern form that allows the Notjeru to be celebrated anew.

Pronunciation Guide

Spellings of Egyptian names and words vary widely, because to date scholars have no set system of converting hieroglyphic and hieratic spellings into our modern alphabet. And because ancient Egyptian, like modern Hebrew and Arabic, leaves out vowel sounds, we cannot know precisely how the language sounded - much as the original pronunciation of ancient Hebrew has also been lost. Make no mistake: the system given below gives no pretensions of 'recreating' ancient forms. Rather, by cross-referencing with Coptic equivalents to replace some of the missing vowels, and by attempting to establish a consistent method of transliterating words, the versions of Egyptian hymns in this book offer the possibility for a modern liturgical form of the Kemetic language.

Vowels:
a = 'ah' sound as in 'falling'
e = 'eh' as in 'let'
i = short 'i' as in 'pick'
o = short 'o' as in 'wonder'
u = long 'oo' as in 'super'

Special sounds:
a' = brief 'ah' with a stop, similar to 'uh-oh'
iu = 'ew' as in 'pew'
kh = throaty 'ch' sound, found in Scottish 'loch' or Jewish 'Chanukah'
ch = called the 'fourth h', similar to German *ich*. Softer than 'kh' sound.
tj = '-tch' as in 'itch'

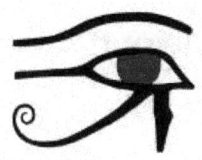

The Notjeru

The Great Ennead – Major Deities

Amun / Amun-Ra

Amon, Ammon, Amen

Major Titles:
Neb Waset - Lord of Thebes
Neb Khau - Lord of Appearances
Nisut Notjeru - King of the Gods (as Amun-Ra)
Neb Ipet-Resyt - Lord of the Southern Residence

Nubian Titles:
Neb Dju Wa'b - Lord of the Pure Mountain
Neb Ipet-Sut - Lord of the Select Place (temple name)

His name meaning "hidden", Amun first rose to widespread prominence during the Middle Kingdom. According to the religious tradition of Thebes and its surrounding areas, Amun represented the ineffable, unknowable force of action and creative power that first brought the world into being. He had a female aspect or counterpart known as Amaunet, but most often His consort was the mother Goddess **Mut**. As Amun merged with **Ra** to become Amun-Ra, a solar-themed Creator, His son by Mut, the lunar deity **Khonsu**, was compared to Horus the Child and to the sun itself. Amun also took on fertility roles, combining with **Min**.

From at least the New Kingdom onward, Amun also took a local form in Nubia at the site of a holy mountain, called 'Pure Mountain' (*Dju Wa'b*) in ancient times but known today as Gebel Barkal. At one end of the flat-topped mountain rises a pinnacle that, to the ancient residents of nearby Napata, resembled a rearing cobra. They regarded this mountain as the birthplace of Amun. Eighteenth-dynasty pharaohs built a temple complex at the site, including one with the same name as Amun's temple at Karnak, *Ipet Sut* ('the most select of places'). By extension, Amun of Napata was considered the southern equivalent to Amun of Thebes. Amun continued to play a major role in Nubian religion, especially state religion, with many kings and queens incorporating His name (as Aman) into their own. Interestingly,

Mut did not remain His sole consort in Nubia; that role sometimes went to **Isis**, or to the more enigmatic goddesses **Anukis** and **Satis**. In a bit of possible cultural exchange, Amun's ram-headed form in Egypt may have been a Nubian contribution. (For more information, see the entry for a ram-headed colleague, **Khnum**.) In the Theban region, Amun's other sacred animal was the Egyptian goose (*Alopochen aegyptiaca*).

Today, Amun continues to represent the transcendent, abstract enigmas of the Divine for His followers. Amun-Ra can be considered His visible manifestation as the sun. Just as in Ramesside times, Amun can also be regarded as the 'Hidden' aspect of a trinity with Ra and **Ptah**, in which Ra represents His image and Ptah His physical body. If this description sounds rather puzzling, that's probably by design; Amun is all about mystery.

Ordinary Egyptians looked to Amun as "Lord of the silent" (meaning those who either don't act contentiously, or who have no public voice) and "Vizier of the poor" who helped the meek and honest over the wealthy and corrupt - themes that are especially poignant today. Another of Amun's avatars known to us from the Late Period tale "The Report of Wenamun" is Amun of the Road. The protagonist of the story took an icon of Amun of the Road with him on his dangerous journey to Phoenicia. Today, this aspect of Amun could act as a guardian of travelers.

Offerings: Amun favors the traditional offerings of bread, beef, water and beer, but also cinnamon, as well as gold (or gold-colored) items and perfumed oils. Frankincense and copal incenses are appropriate 'flavors' to offer Him as well.

Feast Days: Major feasts that involve Amun include Egyptian New Year's, because it marks the birth date of the Creator; the Opet Festival, a multi-day celebration thought to have originated in Thebes; a "Feast of Amun After Opet" (which it's tempting to think of as an 'after party'!); a feast of Amun Entering the Sky (*Aq nu Pet*) in late winter; spring processions in His form of Amun-Min; and the Beautiful Feast of the Valley, in which He crossed the Nile to visit **Hathor** in the Theban necropolis to bring new life to the blessed dead. Several smaller offering and processional observances for Amun occurred throughout the year.

Hymn to Amun from Deir el-Medina

Praise unto Amun-Ra,
I make for Him adoration to His name,
I give Him praises to the height of heaven
And over the breadth of the earth,
I tell His might to travelers north and south;
Beware ye of Him!
Declare Him to son and daughter, to great and small,
Herald Him to generations not yet born;
Herald Him to fishes in the deep, to birds in the sky,
Declare Him to fool and wise,
Beware ye of Him!

You are Amun, Lord of the silent,
Who comes at the voice of the poor;
When I call to You in my distress,
You come to rescue me,
To give breath to him who is wretched,
To rescue me from bondage.

You are Amun-Ra, Lord of Thebes,
Who rescues him in *Duat*;
For You are He who is merciful,
When one appeals to You,
You are He who comes from afar.

(from Miriam Lichtheim's translation of the stela of Nebra)

Liturgical Hymn to Amun From Hibis Temple:

Djed medu in dua' Amun-Ra-Horakhety
Words spoken in worship of Amun-Ra-Horakhety

Djed medu:
Words recited:

Res-ek nofer, Amun-Ra, Horakhety, Atum, Khopri,
May You awake beautifully, Amun-Ra, Horakhety, Atum, Khopri,

Horu djai pet, Bik a'ah zab shuty,
Horus who traverses heaven, Great Falcon, dappled of plumage,

Nofer-her, neb Shuty Ur,
Fair of face, Lord of the Great Twin Plumes,

Res-ek nofer hery tep dua'it im djad-en-ek Notjer temenu.
May You awake beautifully upon the morning (through) that which the entirety of Gods say to You.

Hai hen en-ek im meshru, sua'sh tu kenemut.
Jubilation unto You in the evening, the stars worship You at night.

Sedjer iur dua'it er mosut-ek, khenem-tu muat-ek ra nib.
The Pregnant One lies down in the morning to bear You, Your mother nurses You every day.

Ankh Ra, muet ~~Nik~~!
Ra lives, and ~~Nik~~ [Apophis] dies!

Iu-ek men-tu reqiu-ek kheru,
You are established, while Your rebels are fallen,

Dja'i-ek her-et im ankh, djed, wos nib.
So You might traverse the heavens in all life, stability and dominion.

Uresh-ek im wia'-ek, iu ib-ek nodjem,
You spend the day in Your bark, Your heart being pleased,

Iu Ma'at ka-ti er hat-ek,
Ma'at appearing at Your brow.

Uben Amun-Ra, pesedj Akhety, Kenmet hai khoperu!
As Amun rises, so Akhety shines!

Izet Ra im hay, pet ta' im hay,
The crew of Ra is in jubilation, Heaven and Earth are in jubilation,

Pet ta' im reshresh, Pesdjet a'aht ir-en-ek henu:
Heaven and Earth are in exaltation, The Great Ennead makes acclaim for You:

Amun-Ra Horakhety poru ma'a kheru! (Zap fedu.)
Amun-Ra Horakhety comes forth true of voice! (Four times.)

Osir, Khenty-Amentiu, Notjer a'ah, neb Abju, poru ma'a kheru! (Zap fedu.)
Osiris, Foremost of the Westerners, Great God, Lord of Abydos, comes forth true of voice! (Four times.)

Amun-Hibe, notjer a'ah, user-khopesh, poru ma'a kheru! (Zap fedu.)
Amun of Hibis, Great God, powerful of arm, comes forth true of voice! (Four times.)

Anubis
Anupu, Inpu, Yinepu

Major Titles:
Imi-ut - He in His Wrappings
Neb Ta-Djoser - Lord of the Sacred Land
Tepy Dju-ef - He Over His Mountain
Hery Sesheta - He Over the Secrets

Pop culture has seized upon Anubis' jackal-headed avatar and His role as patron of the embalming arts, but he is most decidedly *not* a gloomy, Egyptian version of the Grim Reaper. (Although a positive view of Anubis' funerary role would be His portrayal in the series adaptation of Neil Gaiman's *American Gods*.) Indeed, Anubis also presides over initiations, which would explain why so many Pagans encounter Him first. Devotees describe Him as a calm, fair listener, which is consistent with His traditional role in conducting the Weighing of the Heart at the deceased's judgment. Interestingly, some of His devotees also recount traumatic childhood experiences that they overcame with His guidance. This seems to reflect an ancient account of Anubis' own origin as the illegitimate son of Nephthys, whom She was forced to abandon but was then raised by Isis. Through this story - which is found in native Egyptian spells as well as Plutarch's account - Anubis could relate easily with children of broken and dysfunctional homes.

In ancient Nubia, Anubis was honored not as patron of embalming - as the practice never really 'caught on' there - but rather as a good shepherd who brought offerings to the deceased.

A fascinating but obscure article builds upon symbolism of Anubis with the lunar disc and connects it to early Coptic art of Saint Christopher, who was often portrayed with a dog's head.

Could the first Copts have equated Anubis with Saint Christopher? The possibility is tantalizing, and may open more avenues for Anubis symbolism in the modern world. Consider that Ellen Cannon Reed, in her book *Circle of Isis*, related how her husband - named Christopher - has Anubis as his patron.

Today, Anubis' patron professions would include not only morticians, post-mortem medical examiners and forensic investigators, but also counselors and social workers. Canines of many forms can act as His symbols; for more information about His traditional jackal/Egyptian wolf form, see the entry on His fellow canine deity **Wepwawet**.

Offerings: Anubis has been known to ask His adherents for steaks. Devotees have also offered Him coffee and chocolates - certainly hazardous foods for ordinary dogs, but then again, Anubis is no ordinary canine.

Feast Days: Anubis plays a major role in the Wagy Feast, the first of three important festivals of the dead that takes place in August. Regional festivals honored Anubis in Denderah, Medinet Habu (or *Djeme*) and elsewhere. Several of His feast days were Robing (also translated "Dressing") observances - which could either refer to ceremonially changing the shawls on His statues, or perhaps wrapping the *Imiut* symbol associated with Him. The festival of "Moving Sand for Anubis" is known from the Middle Kingdom but lacks much historical description; but the idea of dealing with drifting sand suggests it may have involved 'cleansing' rites, sweeping physically and spiritually in honor of Anubis.

Hymn to Anubis:

(adapted from the London-Leiden Papyrus)

Hail and Praise, oh Anupu,
Great God upon Your mountain!
Master of Secrets in Duat,
Ruler of the West,
Fair son of Osir.
Great Physician who heals,
Your seal is our protection.
Crown Prince of the Ennead,
Keen-faced among the Gods,
You stand at Osir's side.
You serve the Blessed Dead,
They live because of You.

Atum

See **Ra.**

Bastet
Bast, Baset, Bahst

Titles:
Irit (en) Ra - Eye of Ra
Nebet Per-Bastet - Lady (or Mistress) of Bubastis
Nebet Ankh-Tawy - Mistress of Ankh-Tawy (ancient city)
Nebet Pet - Lady of the Sky
Notjerit a'aht - Great Goddess

Along with Anubis, Bastet (or Bast) is easily the most famous of Egyptian deities. Cat lovers certainly appreciate Her feline form; but what some of them may not know is that, during earlier periods of pharaonic history, Bastet took the form of a woman with a lioness' (*Panthera leo*) head, much like the goddesses **Sakhmet**, **Mut** and **Tefnut**. Like them, Bastet acted as the Eye of **Ra** who protected the sun god from evil.

Bastet's modern fame has generated numerous misconceptions, especially among mainstream Pagans. One of the more lurid 'urban myths' is that Bastet acts as a patroness of prostitutes, and that if one makes an offering to Her then She is obliged to assist. Like the notion of 'sacred prostitution' itself, which has fascinated critics of polytheism since Old Testament days, this tale about Bastet has no basis whatsoever in fact. It may have been inspired by the Late Period "Tale of Setne-Khaemwaset", in which the protagonist finds himself so desperate to sleep with the beautiful and seductive Tabubu - daughter of a priest of Bastet - that he signs over his entire fortune and the lives of his children just to get in bed with her, only to wake up naked in a street, sporting an embarrassing erection and realizing he'd had a vivid dream. But in an important detail from the story, Tabubu tells Setne-Khaemwaset that she is "not a low person" and rebuffs his offer of money or political favors in exchange for sex. So much for prostitution in the service of Bastet.

Bastet also seems to have played an important role in Nubian religion. She had a temple at the Nubian site of Tare which was visited by Kushite kings as part of their coronation tour. Perhaps the references to Bast in the recent Marvel *Black Panther* film have some legitimate precedent.

Modern worshipers of Bastet look to her as a protective, motherly goddess who loves perfumes and floral scents. She can be at turns playful, generous, or when needs be, a fierce protectress. Being a 'cat person' isn't necessarily required to be Her follower…but it certainly doesn't hurt.

Offerings: Bastet is known to favor dragon's blood incense (particularly in Her protective aspects), in addition to floral varieties. Perfumes and lotions also make suitable offerings. She is reported to like mother-of-pearl glazed items; She may also have a sense of whimsy, asking for stuffed animals as described in the previous chapter.

Feast Days: Besides being honored at New Year's in Her role as Eye of Ra, Bastet has a procession as Mistress of Ankh-Tawy; a shared feast with Sakhmet in late October or November; a Sailing feast in December, where traditionally Her icon was floated on a special barge in Her sacred lake (also called a "Navigation Feast"), and similarly a Feast of Bastet-in-Her-Barque. Two different dates are known for the Feast of "Chewing Onions for Bastet" - but interestingly, onions were not included in major temple offerings for the occasion. Consuming onions was in all likelihood a folk practice that royal endowments did not need to cover, hence their omission in state-sponsored offering lists.

Hymn to Bastet

*(adapted from the Coffin Texts and the
Naos of Bast in Bubastis)*

Inodj har-es Bastet,
Hail and praise unto You, Bastet,

Nebet merit, nebet ankh!
Lady of love, Lady of life!

Sat Atum, Tepy en Neb-er-Djer,
Daughter of Atum, Firstborn of the Lord of All,

Notjerit A'ah, Nebet pet,
Greatest Goddess, Lady of Heaven,

Henut notjeru nibu!
Mistress of all the Gods!
You open the movements of Shu,
For He is Your messenger.
You slaughter with Your arrows,
You slay the Evil One and
Seize the hearts of the wicked foes.
Lady of the Shrine,
Foremost of the Sacred Fields,
Mistress of perfume, Mistress of Joy!
Oh Eye of Horus, Oh Eye of Ra,
Uraeus whom Ra loves,
Protect me [us] until the dawn!

Bes

Bes is typically pictured as a bow-legged dwarf with a shaggy lion's mane and a caricatured human face. His primary functions include fertility and protection, so in ancient art He sometimes wields knives or *sa*-amulets to repel hostile forces. His face also surmounted images of **Horus** the Child on healing plaques known as *cippi* (singular *cippus*). A popular domestic deity, it has been suggested that Bes had roots in Nubia; two of His Egyptian titles were "Lord of Punt" and "Ruler of Nubia", and amulets of Him have been found from Nubia all the way to what is now Israel and Palestine. Interestingly, by the first centuries C.E., Bes took a prominent role as a giver of oracles at the Egyptian holy city of Abydos, in a part of Seti I's temple known as the Memnonion. Even well-to-do Alexandrians were known to make pilgrimages there seeking His guidance. But in 359 C.E., on receiving accusations of subversion, the Roman emperor ordered the Memnonion shut down.

As a giver of fertility and guardian of pregnant women, mothers with infants, children, and ordinary people while they sleep, Bes has nearly universal relevance. He also presides over dancing, music and revelry, aspects noted by modern followers. In *Circle of Isis*, the author's coven members relate Bes as having a keen, if bawdy, sense of humor, and that His most powerful forms of protection come from His gift of laughter. Today Bes' patronage would extend to fertility treatments, maternity wards, nurseries and child care...as well as any party where music is played and jokes are told.

Offerings and festivals - Considerably less information is available on Bes' preferred offerings, and as a historically 'domestic deity' He may not have had official feast days in pharaonic times (though that evidently changed during the Roman era). Music, dancing and revelry have been interpreted as appropriate dedications to Him. Perhaps, as a God of ordinary people who watched over them in their homes, His favorite offerings would be whatever foods His supplicants eat for themselves.

Invoking the Protection of Bes
(from the Papyrus Harris)

Oh Dwarf of Heaven, great dwarf whose head is large, whose back is long, whose thighs are short, great support that reaches from heaven to *Duat*, lord of the great corpse which rests in Iunu, the great living god who rests in Djedu! Pay attention to [N] born of [N]! Guard him [her] by day, watch him [her] by night, protect him [her] as You protect Osiris!

Another Invocation to Bes
(for women seeking pregnancy)

Greatest god of the maternity of women, bounteous god of the maternity of women, planter of female maternity, benefactor of of the maternity of women, sower of the maternity of women, protector of female maternity, guardian of the maternity of women, healer of the maternity of women, father of female maternity, redeemer of female maternity, master of the maternity of women, nourisher of the maternity of women, guardian of the maternity of women, rain of the maternity of women, awakener of the maternity of women, quickener of the maternity of women.

Djehuty (Thoth)

AKA Thoth, Tehuti

Titles:
Sesh Ma'a en Pesdjet - True Scribe of the Nine (Ennead)
Iker en saret - Excellent of Wisdom
Neb Medu-Notjer - Lord of the Sacred Words
Neb Khemenu - Lord of Eight-Town

Djehuty is the native Egyptian name for Thoth, who is often pictured as a man with the head of an ibis (*Threskiornis aethiopicus*), a heron-like wading bird. His other sacred animal is the baboon (*Papio hamadryas*), and in spells He was sometimes addressed as "The Ape". This was not a derogatory name for the ancients, who recognized baboons as extremely intelligent animals - and fittingly, Djehuty is lord of wisdom and intelligence. Inventor of writing, mathematics, magic and medicine, and controller of the lunar phases, today His patronage extends to computers, modern sciences, languages, writing of all kinds and technical arts such as animation. Like his former title of "Ape", which sounds negative but is actually quite positive, today Djehuty is sometimes called the "Nerd" God by followers. Perhaps appropriately, He also is reported to enjoy sweets as offerings. Plutarch observed that worshipers of the Roman era offered honey and figs to Djehuty.

Because our society grows increasingly technical, Djehuty's patronage continues to expand. Students and teachers, scientists and researchers of all types, computer and IT specialists, translators and digital artists all come under His purview. One could even argue that He has an entire new realm under his jurisdiction: cyberspace.

While Djehuty's sacred ibis can be found in zoos - and occasionally in the wild as escapees - around the world, in North and Central America, He can count as a majestic alternative symbol the Great blue heron (*Ardea herodias*).

Offerings: Djehuty is known for His sweet tooth. Figs, honey and pastries would certainly make traditional-style offerings; our modern fig Newtons closely resemble the ancient sweets that would have been offered to Him. Modern candies are also commonly offered. Other traditional gifts to Djehuty are ink and writing implements; today those possible implements are greatly expanded. When I had to replace an old, beloved keyboard that had become obsolete, I dedicated it to Djehuty.

Feast Days: Shortly after New Year's, He is honored at the Djehutet Feast. It was probably the festival that Plutarch described where observers and honey and figs and exclaimed, "A sweet thing is truth!". At His center of worship in Khemnu, he is celebrated for taking a "Solemn Oath" (of what, the Cairo Calendar does not say). He has a Procession festival in mid-winter and an "Appearance" (which in ancient times would have involved His statue) in the modern month of May.

Full Moon Address to Djehuty

Hail, Djehuty, True Scribe of the Ennead,
Who reckons the months, the days, the hours,
Who restores the Sound Eye to fullness.

You return the Eye of Ra
To Her place on the brow of Her father,
And the Ennead of the Gods rejoices.

(adapted from the Book of the Dead)

Hymn to Djehuty

(adapted from a statue of Horemhab, translated by Miriam Lichtheim)

Hail and Praise unto You, oh Djehuty,
Thrice-great God, the son of Ra!
Lord of Khemnu, Wise One in Iunu,
You report to Ra every morning.
Messenger of humankind,
You know people by their speech
And judge them by their deeds.
Those True of Voice before Osir,
Their names are in Your list.

The Ennead gives You praise
As You guide the Bark of Millions,
As You cast out the Evil One,
As You change strife into peace.

You know all secrets, all books, all deeds,
The fleeting moment, the hour of night!
No report to Ra is forgotten,
Your words endure for eternity.
Friend of the people, wise and impartial,
Great One, Lord of Ma'at!

Geb

Sometimes erroneously given as 'Seb'

Notjer A'ah - Great God
Neb tau - Lord of the Lands
It en Diu - Father of the Five

As a masculine embodiment of the earth, Geb contradicts the mainstream Pagan conception of 'Mother Earth'. For the ancient Egyptians, the overarching sky was their Great Mother, **Nut**, while the solid ground on which they stood or rested formed their archetypal father. As father of **Osiris,** Geb shared His association with plant life; the Pyramid Texts describe wheat growing 'from the navel of Geb'. But contrary to the assertions of some modern authors (see my YouTube review of *Temple of the Cosmos* for a good example), Geb is far from a passive element. The ancients regarded earthquakes as His laughter. (He must consider California a funny place.) Geb was also invoked at coronations as a divine ancestor who legitimized new kings. He indeed possesses great energy to support and establish, especially for major undertakings. His is energy so powerful, so patient and steady, that it can be easily overlooked - but don't give Him reason to laugh it off.

Geb's association with the earth lends itself to patronage of geology, seismology and volcanology. But as the ancestral king who ultimately endorsed **Horus** to succeed His father Osiris, Geb could also be invoked in matters regarding wills and successions. One could also seek His blessing and support for new projects, especially long-term ones. Mountains and boulders might seem obvious symbols, but in ancient times the goose was also sacred to Geb, forming the hieroglyph that spells His name. A study of ancient astronomy done in the early 1990's suggested that the constellation we know as Cygnus, the Swan, represented Geb as a goose to the ancient Egyptians, borne aloft by Nut as the Milky Way.

Offerings and feast days - Likely offerings to Geb would include stones or stone objects, especially of materials like sandstone or granite. Woody, 'earthy' incense scents such as pine or cedar would work well. For food offerings, consider grain, particularly bread and beer, and cool water. According to the Cairo Calendar, a feast day celebrating Geb visiting **Anubis** in Busiris (Djedu) was observed on the 2nd of Pa-Rennutet...or on our calendar, February 14th.

Hymn to Geb

(drawn from His titles in the Coffin Texts)

Hail and praise unto You, oh Geb,
Lord of the Lands, Foremost of the Gods!
Lord of Thrones, Father of the Five,
Head of the Dual Enneads;
You judge between the Rivals,
You speak and the Ennead listens.
You endure as the *ba* of the earth,
Your spine is the land that supports us.
You open Your doors for the *akhu*,
Over Osiris do You keep guard.
The earth is purified for You,
Your hands hold up the dawn.
The serpents of the earth, they fear You,
Your *heka* holds them under Your sway.
Governor of the earth, Lord of the *was*-staff,
Support us with Your strength!

Hathor

Hat-hor, Het-hert, Hwt-Hrw

Titles:
Nebet Mehyt - Lady of the North Wind
Nebet Nub - Lady of Gold
Nebet Nuhet - Lady of the Sycamore
Nebet Mafket - Lady of Turquoise

In the science-fiction series *Stargate: SG-1*, Hathor was introduced as the Goddess of "sex, drugs and rock'n'roll". That statement is rather apt, because Hathor is the patroness of love, sexuality, music, and ecstasy. Unfortunately, the Stargate episode went on to depict Hathor as a dangerous seductress, which runs counter to the Goddess' actual nature. Pop culture misinformation strikes yet again.

Hathor presides over not only ecstatic states of all kinds - orgasmic, trance, drug-induced or meditative - but also nursing and motherhood. Milk is sacred to Hathor. Hers is the feminine mystique. Women in ancient times prayed to Her for all manner of concerns, ranging from personal health to childrearing to marital problems and beyond. Men and women alike invoked Her to find a mate. In that vein, today She would preside over dating websites. As Goddess of the West, She welcomed the dead and granted them rebirth; bereaved loved ones probably also turned to Her for comfort as they mourned. But this Goddess of Love also possesses a vengeful aspect, being one of several female deities bearing the title "Eye of **Ra**". Those who act with loving intentions earn Her favor, but those who act with ill intent risk Her wrath.

Today Hathor would be the patroness of musicians and DJ's, couples and those seeking a partner, mothers and mothers-to-be, feminine issues and even feminism as a movement. She is also greatly beloved by adherents in the LGBTQ community, often inspiring them to create moving art and prayers to Her. Their message of acceptance and love in honesty surely resonates with Hathor's.

Offerings: Milk is a powerfully symbolic gift for Hathor. Other traditional offerings to Her include beer, honey cakes (perhaps today honey buns or cinnamon rolls could equate), sistra and the playing of sistra, as well as venison, in recognition of Her lioness aspect as Eye of Ra. Floral and 'sweet' incenses, as well as frankincense and copal (for Her solar aspects) would also be appropriate today.

Feast Days: Hathor enjoyed full festival calendars at both Her center in Denderah, and at the temple of **Horus** at Edfu - and probably other temples now lost to us, such as Ra's complex in Iunu. Thus, our list of feast days to Her is necessarily brief. New Year's was an important observance, in which She reunited with Her father Ra (via bringing Her statues into the noon sunlight). She had a procession, or 'Going Forth', roughly a week afterward, then the Feast of Drunkenness in August. Technically, the entire month of Akhet III, or *Hat-Hor*, was filled with festivals to Her. Late in that month She held a feast day in Kom Ombo (also called 'Ombos'), and on the last day of Her month She had not only a Sailing (or 'Navigation') Feast, but also the Day of 'Revealing the Bosoms of Women'; which in ancient times featured a public procession with a carved wooden phallus - we'll leave it to modern Pagans to decide how to interpret that holiday! She had an often-overlooked role during the Khoiakh Mysteries, even holding another 'Union With the Sun Disc' (or exposure to the sun) in the middle of the week-plus observances. In December comes another Sailing of Hathor; She could be invoked during the Establishing of the Celestial Cow; in spring She is celebrated in Her Creatrix aspect of *Iusa'as*, or the "Hand of Atum", followed by at least two Birth Festivals (Her divine child varying by location). She figures prominently in the

Beautiful Feast of the Valley, in which Amun visits Her desert enclave at Thebes to bring new life to the dead. Later in that month falls a Feast of Eating Cucumbers By the Eye of Horus - see a fuller discussion in the next chapter, under "Observances Then and Now". Multiple procession feasts finish out Her liturgical year. As a major Goddess who was worshipped across Egypt, Hathor truly has a plethora of observances to choose from.

In Praise of Hathor

(Adapted from a Sed Festival hymn)

Come! Make merry for the Golden One,
Good cheer for the Mistress of the Two Lands!
Come! Arise! Come that I may make for You
Rejoicing at twilight and music in the night.
Oh Hathor! You are exalted in the hair of Ra,
In the hair of Ra!
To You is given the sky,
The deep night and the stars!
Great is Her Majesty when She is happy!

Hymn to Hathor

combining New Kingdom love songs and Hathor hymns from Denderah, <u>Ancient Egyptian Literature vols.II</u> and <u>III</u>

Oh Golden One, come to our song
And feast Your heart on dancing!
Shine upon the festival night,
Take joy in seeing the dances!

chorus:
We praise the Golden Goddess
We worship Her majesty
We exalt the Lady of Heaven
Give chanting to our mistress!

Oh come to the procession of revelry,
To the place where we wander the marsh!
Your rites have been established,
Nothing is left for want!

(chorus)

How the beauty of Your face shines
As You appear, O come in peace!
We get drunk looking at You,
Beautiful as gold, O Hathor.
May the waters You provide us
Refresh our mouths and cool our hearts.

(chorus)

Golden One, how good is this song,
Like the song of Horus Himself!
Likewise, see how we dance for You;
Likewise, see how we sing for You!
Give that we may live and prosper!

Horus
Heru, Horu

Titles:
Sa Iset [or *Aset*] - Son of Isis
Nedj-Her-Itef - Defender of His Father
Notjer A'ah - Greatest God
Neb Pet - Lord of the Sky

Worship of Horus dates back to the earliest periods of Egypt's history and was attested across the country. As a result, Horus has a kaleidoscope of attributes and local avatars. As Elder Horus, or *Hor-Ur*, the primeval Lord of the Sky, His eyes are the sun and moon. As the vulnerable Horus the Child (*Hor pa Kherod*), He both embodies and protects all children. In His child aspect, Horus can be identified with fellow Child-Gods **Khonsu** and **Ihy**, and sometimes becomes the son of **Hathor** or **Sakhmet**. Taking the form of a young falcon-headed man as *Hor Sa-Iset*, the 'Son of Isis', He represents courage and the triumph of goodness over evil. In His guise as *Iun-mut-ef* or *Nedj-her-it-ef* ('Pillar of His mother' and 'Defender of His father') He becomes the dutiful son who cares for His parents. More poignantly, anyone who has lost a parent can identify with Horus' position as the son of **Osiris**.

Because Horus was wounded in one eye (or both, depending on the legend) battling His brother/uncle **Seth**, He was often invoked in ancient times to heal eye ailments. In today's world, His patronage might extend to wearers of eyeglasses and contact lenses, those suffering from cataracts, and optometry as a profession. He is also cited among modern Pagans as a protector of servicemen and a patron of martial arts, roles that could also overlap with the fellow falcon-headed god **Montu**. Of course, His role in protecting the young and defenseless has not diminished; perhaps He could be called upon as a much-needed guardian of school children. In personal practice, Horus can be warm and gentle, and extremely effective at casting out hostile entities.

Hawks and falcons - especially the peregrine falcon (*Falco peregrinus*), which is found worldwide - are Horus' quintessential symbol. He can also make His presence known through other species of hawk, such as the red-tailed hawk (*Buteo jamaicensis*) so common throughout North America.

Offerings: Historically, chick-peas (garbanzo beans) were offered to Horus in His aspect as a child; in the Roman Period, terra-cotta figurines pictured Child Horus stirring a pot, which suggested certain foods - perhaps hummus? - were given to children in His name. In His adult aspects, fresh-cooked meat was traditionally offered. It would be best to stick with red meat or poultry: pork is considered taboo to Horus because of its association with His arch-rival Seth. Frankincense, myrrh, sandalwood and copal incenses are all appropriate fragrances.

Feast Days: Like His traditional wife Hathor, Horus has a full liturgical year of feast dates, of which only highlights are covered here. He celebrated numerous Sailing feasts early in the year; as Horus of Behdet, His feast of Sailing at Edfu occurred in late August or September. Like many major Gods, He celebrated feast days at the beginning of a new month, such as at the start of Akhet IV or *Ka-Hor-Ka*. The next month marked the start of growing season and at Edfu, the Coronation of the Sacred Falcon, which celebrated Horus' role as heir to Osiris and king of the living. In January, the Edfu Feast of Victory celebrates His triumph over Seth, and was marked with a sacred drama that has been translated and re-enacted in modern times. In February comes a feast from the region of Kem-Ur, followed by one for the completion (or healing) of His *Udjat* Eye; followed by another feast in late March for the local aspect Horus of Sepa (wherein His mother is Sakhmet). Also in March, the beginning of Shomu (harvest) season marks feasts for two forms of Horus, *Sa-Iset* and *Sema-Tawy*. He then has a 'birth feast' - in essence, a birthday party - as *Hor-Sa-Iset* in Edfu in April; either of these March or April dates could honor His child aspects. Beginning with the new moon in May, Horus and Hathor shared the Beautiful Reunion feast, which combined harvest themes with a conjugal holiday. In early summer, the observance of Eating Cucumbers by the Eye of Horus (see discussion next chapter) would include Him. Not listed on our calendar were several further procession feasts that led up to a major one on the last day of the year. The second of the Days Upon the Year marks Horus' birthday in His Elder aspect - on the Kemetic Reform calendar, it coincides with modern Bastille Day.

Praises of Horus of Behdet

(from His temple at Edfu)

Praise unto You, God of Behdet, Lord of the Sky,
Splendid Winged-Disc who shines in the Horizon,
You beautiful sun who illuminates the darkness,
Splendid child who illuminates the earth,
Iris of the *Udjat* who lights the Two Lands
with His rays!

Fair of face, Hovering one,
Armored, majestic, clothed in gold!
You arise as Khopri when you emerge from *Naunet*,
Your rays spreading over the world -
Shine upon earth as You do in Heaven!

Inodj har-ek Horu, notjer a'ah, neb pet!
Hail unto You, Horus, Great God, Lord of the Sky!

Bik a'ah, sa'b shuty, heqa neteb!
Great falcon, Dappled of Plumage, ruler of flying!

Apy tepy Tawy, sia khnum aton,
Winged disc upon the Two Lands,
sia-falcon united with the sun [disc],

Notjer notjery, bik en nubit!
Holy God, falcon of Gold!

Isis

Aset, Auset, Ast, Iset

Titles:
Uret Hekau - Great of Magic
Mut Horu - Mother of Horus
Notjerit A'ah - Greatest Goddess
Nebet Pet - Lady of the Sky (or 'Mistress of Heaven')

The devoted wife of **Osiris** and mother of **Horus**, Isis is easily among the best-known Egyptian deities today, and scores of modern Pagans venerate Her as their Mother Goddess. Some Kemetics draw a distinction between 'Aset', native name of the Goddess, and 'Isis' as the Hellenized deity worshiped today by mainstream Pagan groups. This remained largely a sectarian difference until the unfortunate confusion with 'Isis' that began in 2014 with a violent Islamist group given an identical-sounding acronym. In any case, the Goddess knows who Her followers are.

Historically, Isis received as much veneration in Nubia as She did in Egypt, and Her worship there continued long after the advent of Christianity in Egypt. In Nubian religious traditions, Isis sometimes acted as the wife of **Amun** or of the native lion-headed god **Apademak**. Her role as a mother goddess resonated with Nubians of all social classes, as it continues to today among adherents in modern traditions such as the Ausar-Auset Society.

A skillful wielder of *heka* (Egyptian magick), powerful healer and eloquent speaker "whose tongue fails not", Isis certainly embodies active feminine qualities. Her patronage would extend to married couples; mothers and their young children; obstetricians and pediatricians; public speakers; and faith- or psychic healers. Some Kemetics report that Isis calls upon them to undertake serious tasks with the expectation that She will not be refused. But the author of *Circle of Isis*, herself a priestess of Isis, described Her as warm, personable and having a definite sense of humor. Other Pagans have reported Isis to be especially helpful and compassionate in times of crisis. On a personal level, several years ago I attended an Isian Imbolc ritual. Their icon for the Goddess was an unprovenanced bronze of Isis seated with Horus in her lap, which had been purchased on the antiquities market - a powerful vessel, and we all felt it. The couple officiating found themselves moved to tears at one point during their opening readings. While we circumambulated the altar further into the ritual, I found myself reflecting on my own troubled experiences with my mother, who showed openly preferential treatment to her sons our whole lives. Seeing an enshrined Goddess with Her son on Her lap recalled painful memories.

Then a voice came, calm but sure. "Did you think that I would not love you?" was all that She said. At that point, I was moved to tears.

I've heard Isis speak to me directly one other time since then, and She was just as steady, gentle and understanding. She does not intrude or make demands. Her love is what a mother's should be - without condition.

Offerings: Isis enjoys flowers and floral-scented incenses, particularly rose, and is also reported to like vanilla fragrances. Traditionally, honey cakes and milk were offered to Her on feast days. As with most Egyptian deities, bread, wine and fruit all make excellent offerings. The two foods considered taboo to Isis since ancient times were fish and pork; though if they were offered out of purely ignorant sincerity, today She would probably be rather forgiving of the oversight.

Feast Days: Following New Year's (which was observed for all the Notjeru), Isis probably played a role in the Wagy Feast, a festival of the dead centering on Her husband Osiris during August. Almost a month later follows the Feast of Isis the Great, followed another month later by 'Isis Goes Forth in Joy'. She shares another Going Forth (or Procession) Feast with Her sister Nephthys in October; but later in the month of Akhet IV (*Ka-Hor-Ka*) the Khoiakh Mysteries mark another somber occasion related to Osiris. In late December or early January the 'Awakening of Isis' is celebrated, and shortly thereafter Isis joins in the Feast of Victory at Edfu for Her son Horus. In spring, She was certainly involved in the lunar-based Birth of Horus *Sa-Iset* ('Son of Isis'). Not listed in our calendar is another feast for His conception - this may have been a bittersweet occasion, as according to legend Isis spent that one night with Her revived husband before He entered the netherworld forever.

In mid-to-late June is the Going Forth of Isis the Brilliant, also known as the 'Aset Luminous' (*Aset Webenut*) Feast. Following the last day of the year (important for probably all deities), Isis celebrated Her birthday on the fourth Day Upon the Year; in Roman times the feast became known as the *Amesysia*. A festival of lights for Isis evolved during Greco-Roman times that is not listed in our calendar: called *Lychnapsia*, it took place on August 11 or August 12 according to the Roman calendar.

Hymns to Isis From Philae

Philae Hymn III:
A'set uret, muat-Notjer, nebet Aiu-rek,
Isis the Great, mother of the God, Lady of Philae,

Hemet-notjer, duait notjer, djohret-notjer,
God's wife, God's adorer, God's hand,

Muat-notjer, hemet-nisut uret,
Mother of God, Great Queen,

Sekeret, nebet chekeru ahet.
Adornment, Lady of Ornaments of the shrine.

Nebet a'bu a'kha'khet
Lady and desire of the green fields,

Aimety meh ahet im noferu-es,
Nursling Who fills the shrine with Her beauty,

Aidet ahet, henut reshut,
Fragrance of the shrine, mistress of joy,

Aitjyt geset im sut-notjeryt.
Who runs Her course in the Sacred Place.

Aigepet urekh im sekhed-es,
Raincloud that greens the fields when She descends,

Sherit benrit merut, henut net Shemau Mehu,
Maiden, sweet of love, Mistress of Upper and Lower Egypt,

Airet medu in chenu Pesdjet.
Who issues orders among the Ennead.

Airyt-pa't, uret hesut, nebet ia'met,
Princess, great of praise, lady of charm,

Khonem-es khent-es teftef im antjiu wa'dj.
Whose face loves the trickle of fresh myrrh.

Philae Hymn IV:
Netes sety Hapi
She is the One who pours out the Inundation,

Airi ankh heru-nib sekhoper wa'djua'dj.
Which makes all people live and green plants grow.

Rdi-et hotepu-notjer en Notjeru,
Who provides sacred offerings for the Gods,

Poret em kheru en akhu.
And voice offerings for the *Akh*-spirits.

Her-nety netes Nebet Pet,
Because She is Lady of Heaven,

Tja'y-es im Neb Duat,
Her husband is Lord of *Duat*,

Sa-es im Neb Ta';
And Her son is Lord of the Land;

Tja'y-es im wa'b ronpy-ef im Senemut er ter-ef.
Her husband is the pure water, renewing Himself
at Biggeh at His time.

Netes Nebet Pet, Ta', Duat,
She is Lady of Heaven, Earth and *Duat*,

Her sekhoper-sen en qema't-en ib-es in irit-en awy-es,
Having brought them to being through what Her heart
conceived and Her hands created,

Ba pu nety im niut nibut,
She is the *Ba* which is in every city,

Up-har-es hena sa-es Hor, sen-es Osir.
Watching over Her son Horus, and Her brother Osiris.

source: "Six Hymns to Isis at Philae" by L. V. Zakbar

Khopri

Khepri, Xepri
See **Ra**.

Khnum

Khnoum, Chnoum

Khnum hails from the southern region of the First Cataract, though in early periods His worship may have been more widespread; the famous Fourth Dynasty king Khufu's name is actually a shortening of *Khnum-kuefui*, "Khnum protects me". It's also theorized that Khnum originated in Nubia because of His ram-headed avatar, which is one of two now-extinct types of barbary sheep, *Ovis longipes paleoaegyptiacus* (which had twisted horns that went out straight to either side) or *Ovis platyura aegyptiaca* (whose horns curled over, similar to an American bighorn sheep - think of the truck emblem). Rams figured prominently in Nubian culture, which depended on herding more so than in Egypt.

A creator whose name means "to join, unite", Khnum fashions Gods and men on His potter's wheel. At the island of Elephantine, He oversaw the annual Nile floods with the help of **Anuket** and **Satit**. His powers of fertility nourished the fields and brought bountiful crops. Further north at Esna, he formed a joint Ennead - Greek name for a family of Gods, typically nine - with the Creatrix **Neith**. Khnum could fiercely fight the forces of evil as well, combining with **Ra** or **Shu** to defeat His enemies.

Today, Khnum acts as a kindly personal patron, and His followers find Him to be a creativity-inspiring patron of artistry and crafts - not just His traditional ceramics, but other handicrafts, even including origami. Khnum can also be invoked for matters of physical health, fertility, or perhaps prosthesis (though here, His patronage might overlap with **Ptah**'s). One follower also reports honoring Khnum on Father's Day, in light of His role as Creator.

Offerings: Khnum reputedly prefers "mellow", soothing fragrances and subtle, earthy incense flavors. Soups, teas and non-spicy food offerings work well. Offering dishes and cups of ceramic ware are also appropriate - especially handmade ones.

Feast Days: Following New Year's, Khnum shares a feast with Anuket in September (and may have been involved in a feast for Anuket and Satit a week-and-a-half later). In late January or early February, "The Gods Make Way For Khnum". On the first of Poret IV, or *Pa'en-Rennutet*, Khnum celebrated a festival that combined elements of Lifting the Sky (see Shu and Ptah for further description) and a celebration of the Potter's Wheel, in which Khnum endows His creative powers to all female beings. The Eye of Ra as mother of humanity and the birth of a divine child (an aspect of **Horus**) were also celebrated then. In April, He shares a Going Forth with Neith at Esna that involved execration rites using fishes (certain species were considered unclean) burned at the temple gates. In June came an Appearance festival that had a dramatic participation element; Khnum's statue spent the night in a special enclosure, outside of which no torches or unclean servants were permitted. The next day marked 'Grasping the Crook' (also translated 'Taking Up the Club'), where participants engaged in a mock battle against the forces of chaos that, in ancient times, may have been bloody affairs! Later in June, Khnum celebrates a feast as Khnum-Ra, in which He decrees that **Nut** shall not give birth during that same month as His birthday (perhaps inspiring Plutarch's story about the Epagomenal Days). Finally, a great procession and lighting of torches marked the last day of the year.

Not listed in our calendar was a feast on Apip 9, or late May/early June, in which Khnum is identified with Ra, His statue taken to a special enclosure and turned to face inward. Meanwhile Shu - via priests and participants making noise outside the sanctuary - defended Him from evil, before Khnum returned safely to His usual home.

(The following hymn draws from a morning hymn to Khnum, translated by Lichtheim; if you wish to use it for a morning address,

add "Awake in peace" to the beginning of each stanza and "Awake peacefully" after each semicolon.)

Hymn to Khnum From Esna

Khnum-Amun, the Ancient One,
Issued from Nun;

Lord of the fields, Great Khnum,
Who makes His domain in the meadow;

Lord of Gods and men,
Lord of the war cry;

Mighty planner,
Great power of Egypt;

Lord of life,
Wooer of women,
To whom come Gods and men as He bids;

Ram, Great of majesty,
Tall of plume, sharp of horn;

Great lion,
Slayer of rebels;

Crocodile-king,
Mighty victor,
Who conquers as He wishes;

Leader of herdsmen,
Who grasps the staff,
Smiting His attacker;

Shu, Strong of arm,
His father's champion,
Slayer of rebels;

Fighting ram who chases His foes,
Herdsman of His followers;

Multi-formed One,
Who changes shape at will;

Khnum, who fashions as He wishes,
Who sets every man in his place!

Khonsu
Khons, Chonsu

Titles:
Pa cherod - The Child
Tepy en Amun - Firstborn of Amun
A'ah ur - The Very Great
Nisut cherodu nibu - King of all children
Pa' Ir Sekheru - Maker of Plans

A lunar deity with some solar attributes as well, Khonsu is the child of **Amun** and **Mut**; or in Memphis, the son of **Ptah** and **Sakhmet**, and in Kom Ombo, of **Hathor** and **Sobek**. Like many Egyptian deities, Khonsu's nature is multi-faceted. The Pyramid Texts mention Him as a frightful punisher of the wicked and a controller of fate, but His titles from the Greco-Roman period include "good youth, sweet of love" and even "king of all children". A magical spell from this same time period instructs users to enshrine an image of Khonsu-the-Child in their home or business to attract good fortune. Like His fellow lunar god **Djehuty**, with whom He can combine, Khonsu sometimes takes the form of a hamadryas baboon. He could also appear as a hawk-headed man or a young child in mummy-like swaddling wrappings, wearing a braided sidelock of youth.

Modern Pagans have also found Khonsu to be a protective, friendly and beneficent God who chases away negative forces, bringing peace and wisdom to His supplicants. True to His child aspect, Khonsu is also reported to enjoy games. Today, as in ancient times, He would be a patron of children and the things they enjoy.

Offerings: Silver and blue or pale-colored stones (especially moonstone) are associated with Khonsu. He is reported to prefer calming fragrances - "nothing too pungent", according to one follower - and juniper. He also appreciates sweet bread and fruits, games and toys.

Feast Days: Aside from New Year's and the last day of the year, or Day of *Mosyt*, Khonsu also joined Mut (as did **Bastet**) in Her 'Sailing' festival in early winter. But Khonsu's biggest festival season occurs during the month bearing His name. A feast on both the first day of *Pa-Khonsu* and the last day, plus a "Going Forth of Khonsu" in what is now April, celebrated His birth and the good fortune He can bestow. As a lunar deity, He is honored at the New Moon and First Crescent especially.

To Khonsu the Child
Drawn from epithets used in temples and private monuments

Khonsu pa cherod, a'ah ur, tepy en Amun,
Khonsu the Child, very great, firstborn of Amun,

Hunu nofer, bener merut, nisut cherodu nibu!
Goodly youth, sweet of love, King of all children!

Khy ankh mosut, uhem mosut mi aton,
Babe born alive, Who repeats birth like the sun [disc],

Uhem ronep en Ra im Wa'set.
Who repeats the renewal of Ra in Thebes.

Khy im dua'u, nekhekh im mesher,
Babe in the morning, old man in the evening,

hunu ronep ir tep-teru,
youth who renews at the proper times,

ii im shet im-khut ketket-ef.
who arrives as an infant after His old age.

Hemes-en-es su im Wa'set in shefy shopes,
Whom She [Mut] gave birth to in Thebes as the august child,

ankh im khoperu-ef en Khopri,
the Living One in His manifestation of Khopri,

Ra uhem-en-ef moskhau,
Ra after He repeated births,

Atum im mesher im khent ro Manu.
Atum in the evening within the entrance of Manu.

Djefedj en Udjat, Horu im hunu ronep,
Iris of the *Ujdat*, Horus as a young child,

Khy en Amun-Ra.
Babe of Amun-Ra.

Neb ka'u, asha' djefa'u,
Lord of food, plentiful of sustenance,

Neb cheru di en mer-ef!
Lord of offerings who gives to those He loves!

Ma'at is both a concept and a specific Goddess. Both metaphorically and personally, *ma'at*/Ma'at comes from the Creator (or Creatrix). Thus, She is the daughter of **Ra**, **Amun**, **Ptah** or **Neith**. Embodying the correct natural order of the universe, which includes truthfulness and righteous action, She sustains the Gods who in turn sustain the world. Her symbol is the feather, particularly the ostrich feather. Its airiness implies that misconduct and disorder are burdens, whereas a life lived in accord with Her is light and free - hence the Egyptian belief that one's heart would be weighed in final judgment against Her feather. But truth is sometimes painful. All of the Eye of Ra Goddesses, known for Their searing flame and vengeful lion forms, could be identified with Ma'at.

The concept of *ma'at* is central to modern Kemetic beliefs, even though they may sometimes disagree over its specific application. The Goddess Ma'at was invoked historically by Egyptian tribunals; today, She would continue to preside over legal matters. The familiar Western symbol of Lady Justice holding the scales - itself a holdover from Roman paganism - could easily find re-interpretation as a symbol of Ma'at. Today, She is also invoked as one of the Four Virtues of Ra; see "The Little Ennead" for Her fellow Virtues, **Heka**, **Hu** and **Sia**.

Offerings: For Ma'at, these would include the traditional Egyptian offerings of baked bread and cool water. Light incense fragrances and feathers would also apply, but treat feathers as symbolic; good deeds and honest conduct are Ma'at's greatest offerings.

Feast Days: During our month of October, a holiday honors Ma'at being raised up to Ra; certain symbolic and ritual actions were doubtless performed historically, but the greater meaning of performing works of good still holds now as then. This theme was repeated with another day of Raising Ma'at in early winter (month of *Makhir*). But some entries from the Cairo Calendar do not suggest festive occasions; in late May, one date alludes to strife between Ma'at and the other Gods, then a few days later "Ma'at and Ra go forth in secret", and people were advised not to go out that day. Those dates are not included on our calendar, as they would not be observable holidays. However, one partially damaged entry, for what would be June 14, describes Ma'at and the Gods performing rites. While not included in our main list of feast days due to space (that date being already noted for the Procession of Isis the Brilliant One), it would be another appropriate day to honor Ma'at.

Address to Ma'at

(adapted from the Hibis Temple texts)

Hail and praise unto You, oh Ma'at,
Shining upon the brow of Ra!
You brought forth the Gods from Yourself,
You brought peace unto the Two Rivals.
The Lord of All, He lives through You,
You provide for His house every day.
May You build Your magnificent throne
On our heads, in our mouths, in our hearts!

(See also the Litany to Ma'at and Ra *in "Special Readings for Holidays".)*

Min

Sometimes rendered incorrectly as 'Amsu'

Titles:
Ka Mut-ef - Bull of His Mother
Qai Shuty - Tall of Plumes
Sa Osir - Son of Osiris
Mos-en Iset - Born of Isis

Min leaves little to the imagination, unless His image has been censored - which, in the early days of Egyptology, happened frequently. Pictured as a man in mummy wrappings wearing a bonnet with tall, twin plumes, He holds a flail in one hand and His outlandishly erect phallus in the other. Modern Pagans have certainly seized upon this theme, looking to Min as a God of sexuality, especially male. Male potency drugs such as Viagra would surely come under His purview, and modern worshipers have been known to offer Him 'adult toys' of the male variety. (Historically, though, votive phalli were offered to **Hathor** in the hundreds.)

But in ancient times, Min's 'male potency' served for more than just recreation and procreation. He combined with **Amun** to represent the latter's creative potency. In His harvest festival, Min represented the passing of roles from father to son, embodied by **Osiris** passing his throne to **Horus**. During the ritual, Min's consort was identified as **Isis**, which is reflected in the modern Pagan motif of the God who engenders Himself through His mother. Once identified with Horus, "Strong of Arm", Min is hailed as a powerful deity who puts an end to strife. His flail, as well as His impressive member, are meant to chase away evil.

Interestingly, even into recent times Egyptian farmers would place carved phallic figures in their fields to protect the crops - harking back to Min's statue being carried in procession through local fields to bless the crops. Outside of Egypt, though,

Min might raise a few eyebrows if His image were used as a scarecrow! And of course, in modern times, Min's patron professions would probably include porn actors of all persuasions. But His role in protecting and blessing the fruits of the field extends His patronage to farmers, field workers, and animal husbandry.

Offerings: Grain and especially Cos (romaine) lettuce are traditional fare for Min. Myrrh, especially sweet myrrh, is historically His preferred incense. As mentioned above, adult novelty items have become common offerings as well.

Feast Days: Min probably celebrated festival processions in ancient times for major seasonal events such as New Year's, the beginning of winter (or planting season) and the beginning or end of each month. But at Sais, He celebrated a feast day in late December/early January, followed by a 'Going Forth' at Coptos later in January. In late winter He celebrated a feast of 'Going to His Festival Tent', which is suggestive of what might have been done to observe the occasion (the Cairo Calendar also directs users to "smell sweet myrrh"). As Amun-Min, He held important 'Going Forth' at the first of summer, marking the official start of the harvest season, then an 'Appearance' at Esna. On the last day of *Pa-Khonsu*, Min celebrated another harvest-themed festival that probably lasted into the first day of the next month. In the last month of the year, He celebrated another feast at Akhmim, then one more near the end of the year.

Hymn to Min

(adapted from the stela of Sobek-iry, translated in <u>Ancient Egyptian Literature vol. I</u>)

Adoration to Min, to Horus praise;
He with His arm upraised!
Hail Min in His going forth,
Lofty of Plumes,
Son of Osiris, Born of Isis.
Great in the Dual Shrines,
Mighty in Ipu, You of Gebju.
Horus the strong-armed,
Lord of reverence
Who brings pride to silence,
Sovereign of the gods!
Fragrant when He comes from Medja-land,
You of Utent, hail and praise!

Mut

Titles:
Nebet Tawy - Mistress of the Two Lands
Nebet Isheru - Mistress of the Sacred Lake
Notjerit A'ah - Greatest Goddess
Nebet Pet - Lady of the Sky

One of Mut's roles is encompassed in the meaning of her name: 'Mother'. Hymns describe Her travelling across Egypt to give birth to **Khonsu**, and thus the light (which also puns Khonsu's name, the 'Traveler'). But Mut is much more complex than a mother archetype. She also wears the dual crown and acts as Queen of the Gods to **Amun**'s King of the Gods. In *Great Goddesses of Egypt* author Barbara Lesko describes Her as a 'wise crone' more concerned with civic affairs; while some of the book's other conclusions seem rather questionable, this aspect of Mut could carry some legitimacy in Pagan interpretations. One follower described Her as capable of being "a beautiful motherly woman, a fierce and sensual feline, or a patient and watchful vulture" - lionesses and Egyptian vultures (*Neophron percnopterus*) both being animals associated with Her in ancient times. And while strict Kemetics may eschew the idea, Mut could potentially adapt to mainstream Paganism's triune Goddess aspects of Maiden (as the daughter or Eye of **Ra**, one of Mut's aspects), Mother and Crone (as Creatrix, another historical aspect of Mut). Indeed, flexibility may be one of Mut's greatest attributes.

Offerings: As a Mother Goddess, milk and honey cakes were traditionally offered to Mut. Flowers and beer were offered to her as an Eye of Ra Goddess. Today, possible incense flavors include frankincense, sandalwood, copal and dragon's blood. Citrus scents and flavors are considered by many Pagans to be appropriate for solar deities, such as Eyes of Ra. Some also offer sweets.

Feast Days: Besides New Year's, Mut also partook in feasts to Amun as part of His Ennead, or family of local Gods. In Thebes, She was identified with **Sakhmet** and honored with much beer at the Feast of *Tekhy*, or Drunkenness, in August. At the end of *Ta'Ibet*, or around mid-December, she celebrated a 'Sailing' festival; in ancient times this meant Her statue was floated in a special boat on Her *Isheru* lake, accompanied by **Bast** and **Khonsu**. (The popular New Kingdom personal name *Mutemwia*, or 'Mut in Her Boat', may have referred to this festival.) She also celebrated during the birth feasts for Khonsu during His eponymous month. During the Feast of the Valley in Thebes, She joined Amun and Khonsu in travelling across the river to Deir el-Bahari temple. Finally, in June, she celebrates another holiday as 'Mut of Isheru'.

Hymn to Mut:

(From the Crossword Hymn)

Praise unto Mut, Lady of Heaven,
Mistress of Amun's house!
Lovely of hands, She shakes Her sistra,
Her sweet voice is pleasant to the heart!
She illumines the world with Her rays,
She causes all lands to prosper.
Unique One without equal,
Eternity belongs to Her.
Great One in Heaven, Great of dread,
Foremost in the Ennead,
Mistress of the Two Lands,
Who shines on all faces like Ra!

*(Note to intrepid readers: the following Egyptian-language hymn uses a different spelling of 'Mut' for a particular reason. Refer to the entry for **Nut** for an explanation of this spelling.)*

Adoration of Mut:
(From Her temple reliefs in Karnak)

Dua Muat, uret, nebet Isheru,
Adoration of Mut, the Great, Mistress of Isheru,

mosut shuu im-uhem im Waset,
Who gives birth to light again in Thebes,

khons-et Tawy beka'tu im aton,
Who traverses the Two Lands pregnant with the sun,

di-es er ta' im-ef im Hat-Muat.
that She may give birth to Him in the Temple of Mut.

Tema't en Ra, qema't shuu,
Mother of Ra, She who creates light,

mehenet uret debenet it-es Ra,
great Uraeus who encircles Her father Ra,

di su er ta' im Khonsu,
who gives birth to Him as Khonsu,

Sa't tema't, irit qema' sey!
[both] Daughter and Mother,
who makes Her own Creator!

Neith
Nit

Titles:
A'aht - The Great
Nebet pet - Mistress of the sky
Nebet ankh - Mistress of life
Up-Waut - Opener of the Ways
Mut Ra - Mother of Ra

Neith tends to get short shrift in literature on Egyptian deities. She is often described as simply 'a war goddess who is also a creator', who also happens to preside over weaving. Two reasons probably contribute to this all-too-summary description: one is traditional academic disinterest in Goddesses (and mortal women). The other is a language barrier, as nearly all of the major studies of Neith were written in French and have yet to be translated into English. Fortunately for our purposes, though, *je peux lire en français.*

Neith is one of the oldest Egyptian deities. Evidence of Her worship spans from the early Dynastic period to the first centuries C.E., a time frame of roughly three thousand years. She was hailed as the great Creatrix who existed before time and brought everything into being, the 'Mother of Ra' as well as His Eye. Her other celebrated son was the crocodilian **Sobek**, and Neith could be pictured nursing twin crocodiles (which brings the idea of teething and painful nursing to an entirely new level!). She was especially identified with Mehet-Uret, 'The Great Flood', which was a bovine embodiment of the primeval waters. In Memphis, She was called 'North of Her Wall' because She had a temple on the north side of the city that corresponded to Ptah 'South of His Wall'. She brought fertility to the fields, presided over the spoken word, and acted as a patroness to perfume- and medicine-making as well as mining precious stones (which She shared in common with **Hathor**, including the title

'Mistress of Malachite'). But She most definitely possessed a fierce side: Her name is thought to mean, 'Terrifying One', which is homonymous with the word for the Lower Egyptian red crown She typically wears. She overlapped roles with **Sakhmet**, including in commanding the "Arrows", demonic messengers that caused plague and misfortune. The nome standards for the two districts near and around Sais, the Delta center of Her worship, featured a pair of arrows crossed over a shield - epitomizing the 'Mistress of the Bow' and 'Regent of the Arrow'. But just as "life and death are in Her hand," as the temple texts at Esna extol, Neith also received and protected the dead. In funerary contexts, She took the title *Nebet Amentet*, 'Mistress of the West', another She shared with Hathor. Paired with **Duamutef**, She protected the stomach of the deceased.

With today's renewed interest in Goddesses, Neith deserves to reclaim Her place of prominence. She has historical roles that correspond to all three aspects of the mainstream Triple Goddess ("Maiden-Mother-Crone"), but even from a strictly Kemetic perspective, She still has much to offer. She can preside over chemistry, pharmaceuticals - surely a field that could benefit from Her guidance - women in law enforcement and the military; and leaders of all genders, as Neith Herself was described as 'part masculine'. (This level of androgyny could extend Her patronage to transgendered and genderfluid individuals.) Neith also possesses great power to protect; while She was said to have engendered the evil serpent A'apep, She is also described as having the power to destroy him utterly.

Offerings: Oils and perfumes, milk and cool water all make appropriate offerings for Neith. As for incense, She seems to favor 'spicy' scents; so, in addition to frankincense and myrrh, offer cinnamon, clove, or dragon's blood (or combinations thereof). Her associated colors are deep red or red and blue-green in combination. Real bows and arrows are expensive nowadays, but could certainly be consecrated to Her. Because of Her associations with the Eye of Ra and warfare, meat offerings would be suitable, but avoid pork and fish especially; the Nile perch (*Lates niloticus*), a freshwater fish capable of reaching six feet in length, was considered sacred to Neith. Study, learning and personal betterment in Her service are also much-appreciated offerings.

Feast Days: Following the general New Year festivities, Neith received a visit from Elder Horus in mid-August, then celebrated a feast in September at Esna temple. In late September, She shared a festival with Her son **Tutu** at Esna; in late October at Sais, She held a six-day-long 'Appearance' feast that involved a procession, hymns and offerings. During the Khoiakh (Osiris) Mysteries at Esna, She celebrated a Union with the Sun Disc and 'opening of Her palace', presumably to let in recharging sunlight. In December, at roughly the same time that other Eye Goddesses celebrated Sailing festivals, Neith observed a similar Sailing on Her sacred lake (called the *Acher*) at Esna. Her son **Heka**, the 'Child of Sais', also participated. In late December (or early January) She held two more feasts at Her temple in Sais: first the 'Opening the Doors of the House of Neith', in which the main temple gates opened for a procession and bountiful food offerings were distributed, then a Going Forth in which She is joined by Sobek. The Cairo Calendar says of this feast date - which, on the Kemetic Reform calendar, would be December 25 - that She takes writing materials with Her and that "You will see good from Her hands".

Two more feasts centered in Sais follow in January, including a nocturnal 'Going Forth' that was specifically said to last for four hours. Secret rites, perhaps involving execrations, were probably performed then. Following another Saite festival on the first of *Pa'en-Rennutet*, Neith had another sailing feast in Esna that celebrated Her son Heka (who evidently played the role of Child God parallel to **Khonsu** or **Horus**), the birth of Ra, and the birth of Horus at the appearance of the lunar crescent. In

April, Neith shared an observance with **Khnum** at Esna which involved secret execration rites at the four doors to a sacred enclosure, followed by feasting. Three weeks late came a 'Revealing the Face' holiday similar to New Year's and the 'Opening the Doors. She had one last major feast in late May that commemorated how She saved Ra from the crocodiles by lifting Him above the waters; this one involved asperging Her sacred plaza in Esna with unguents and a public procession. Like most major deities, She would have partaken in processions and feasting at the end of the year as well.

Hymn to Neith

(drawn from Her titles in Esna and Sais)

Hail unto You, Oh Neith, the Great,
The One who existed before existence,
You who made all that is, Who created all that exists!
Eldest of the Primeval Gods, Fashioner of Ra,
Mother of Ra who was at the Beginning!

Unique One without equal,
Mistress of Destiny, Regent of Fortune,
Earth is under Your command,
One does not make plans without Your knowledge.
Queen of the Gods in Heaven,
Sovereign of the Gods in the Earth;
Mistress of the Bow, Regent of the Arrow,
Who keeps the Arrow-demons under Your authority.
Mistress of great fear,
Who created the Twin Crocodiles,
Life and death are under Your supervision.

You fill sky and earth with Your beauty,
Light the Two Lands with the rays of Your eyes,
You encompass Your son as
the light of the Two Lands!

Father of fathers, who makes fertile
the seed of Gods and men,
Great Cow who nourishes all things,
Mother of mothers who is like no other!

Nephthys
Nebet-hat, Nebet-het

Titles:
Nebet Notjeru - Mistress of the Gods
Nebet ankh - Mistress of Life
Notjerit a'ah - Greatest Goddess
Nebet pet - Mistress of the Sky

Nephthys is the twin sister of **Isis** and sister-wife of **Seth**, sometimes described as the 'dark alter ego of Isis'. By far the most common historical references to Nephthys, whose native name *Nebet-Hat* means 'Lady of the House' or 'Mistress of the Temple', have to do with Her shared mourning with Isis over the body of **Osiris**. Together the twin sisters grieved Osiris' death, helped to prepare Him for mummification, guarded Him in the Underworld and raised His son **Horus**, with Nephthys acting as a wet-nurse, or perhaps as a doting and protective aunt. In spells for protection (of both the dead and asleep), Nephthys acts as one of the Four Noble Ladies. In guarding the lungs of the deceased, She pairs with **Hapi**.

Nephthys' relationship with Her husband Seth was turbulent. She was said to have cheated on Him by tricking Osiris into bed with Her, thus conceiving **Anubis**. While our main source of this story comes from Plutarch, the Greek author writing in Roman times, a spell preserved in Old Coptic also refers to the episode, suggesting it was a native Egyptian story. Nephthys' sisterly bond with Isis was unaffected by the affair, and ultimately Her loyalties remained with Isis and Osiris rather than Her own husband. This idea of a loveless marriage between Nephthys and Seth has certainly resonated with modern Pagans. By its extension She could easily act as an intercessor for partners in broken or abusive relationships, or as patroness of those who work to assist survivors of domestic violence. Lastly, in the book *Circle of Isis*, Nephthys is identified with the dark phase of the moon, and described as a Lady of Mystery who teaches through indirect means.

Offerings: One Independent Kemetic suggested a link between Nephthys and the enjoyment of beer; scholarship on the connection is currently not known. Rose and sandalwood incenses, which are enjoyed by Her sister, could be offered to Nephthys as well; in fact, a number of Kemetics have observed that They share similar tastes in offerings.

Feast Days: Somber days for Isis are also somber occasions for Nephthys. But They share a 'Day of Joy' in the month of October, before playing major roles in the Osiris Mysteries. It would be safe to conclude that festivals for Osiris of Abydos 'and His Ennead' would include Nephthys as well. But Her birthday is easy to remember: as the last of the Days Upon the Year, it falls the day before Egyptian New Year's.

The following invocation comes from a spell meant to protect a bedroom and includes Nephthys as one of the 'Four Noble Ladies' alongside Her sister Isis, plus Neith and Serket.

From a spell for "Protection of the House":

"In the name of the Four Noble Ladies, I encircle this room and this bed. Their flame is in their mouths and their fire goes behind them to chase away any male enemy, any female enemy, any male dead, any female dead, any demons who seek to enter. They shall not enter in the day, they shall not enter in the night, they shall not enter at any time. They shall be turned back by the Four Noble Ladies, whose flame is in their mouths and whose fire goes behind them."

Nut
Nuit

Titles:
Netjeret A'ah - Great Goddess
Nebet Pet - Lady of the Sky
Mut Netjeru - Mother of the Gods
Kha Bauet - She of a Thousand Ba's

Daughter of **Shu** and **Tefnut** and a powerful mother Goddess in Her own right, Nut embodies the sky, or more specifically (according to recent research) the Milky Way. Artistically, Nut appears as a nude woman with arms and legs outstretched, often arching over Her husband **Geb**, who forms the earth. She plays a crucial role in the Egyptian view of the afterlife; the deceased hoped to enter Her womb, where they could be reborn with the sun each day, or else become one of the 'Imperishable Stars' (circumpolar stars that are visible year-round) within Her celestial body. Nut could also be identified with **Hathor** as a Goddess emerging from a tree to offer shade, cool water and nourishment to the dead.

Nut also took the form of the Celestial Cow, essentially Her same role as vault of the heavens but pictured as a star-spangled cow held aloft by **Shu**. This form comes into play as part of the tale of Destruction of Mankind, in which **Ra** leaves earth for the sky following a rebellion by humanity that is put down by **Sakhmet**, nearly annihilating humankind in the process.

Understanding how Nut is related to other Gods illustrates the difficulty of treating Their stories literally. As daughter of Shu, Nut is technically Ra's granddaughter; but in the solar cycle, She takes Ra into Her body at sunset and gives birth to Him at dawn, acting as His mother. Plutarch, writing during the Roman era, related that Nut could not give birth on any day of the year, thus **Djehuty** played a board game with the moon (today interpreted as **Khonsu**) to win five extra days in which Nut could give birth to Her children - **Osiris**, **Horus** (who was also son of Osiris!), **Seth**, **Isis** and **Nephthys**. This explained the five Days Upon the Year (Epagomenal Days), but it was probably not meant to explain precise family relationships among the Egyptian Gods - at least not in the Egyptians' eyes, as they lacked a specific word for 'grandfather' or 'grandmother'.

Sadly, today light pollution makes viewing the Milky Way difficult for many people, hiding Nut and Her vault of stars. Our modern understanding of astronomy could suggest a different role for Nut as earth's protective veil of mesosphere, or what we now call the Van Allen Belts that block out space radiation. Spiritually, Nut acts as a personal patroness for some independent Kemetics. As 'Nuit', Nut is identified as the primeval Mother Goddess in Thelemic tradition.

Offerings: As a mother Goddess, milk and honey cakes were traditional offerings to Nut that would still hold relevant today. (Again, the modern form of honey cakes may vary.) For specific incense offerings, try frankincense, myrrh, or lavender. For physical objects, deep blue or blue with gold accents are colors especially associated with Nut. Of course, another excellent way to honor Nut would be to go stargazing.

Feast Days: Nut is honored in the December feast of Establishing the Celestial Cow; in midwinter She has another Feast, as the one 'Who Counts the Days'. She may have played a role in the Feast of Lifting the Sky, observed at various points in the winter season, as well as during the Days Upon the Year, in which She gave birth to Her five children.

As often as the ancient texts mention Nut, their references prove too sparse to condense into a full hymn; and no historical litanies to Nut survive. But a practice from modern Hinduism called archana, *or the chanting of names of a deity (often totaling 108 in their practice), can provide us with a solid starting point for Nut and some of Her fellow Goddesses. Readers may also notice that 'mother' in Egyptian is rendered atypically here. That allows us to distinguish between the otherwise identically-spelled words - both transliterated as* mwt *- for 'mother' and 'vengeful dead', both of which occur elsewhere in the same litany. Clues from Coptic, which spells 'mother' as μααυ, give us our educated guess of* muat, pronounced 'mwooaht'.

Chant for Nut

Dua Nut, a'aht
Adoration of Nut, the Great

Dua Nut, nebet pet
Adoration of Nut, Lady of the Sky

Dua Nut, muat Notjeru
Adoration of Nut, Mother of the Gods

Dua Nut, notjery
Adoration of Nut, the Divine

Dua Nut, notjerit a'aht
Adoration of Nut, Great Goddess

Dua Nut, muat Ra
Adoration of Nut, Mother of Ra

Dua Nut, muat siba'u
Adoration of Nut, Mother of the Stars

Dua Nut, kha bauet
Adoration of Nut, She of a Thousand *Ba*'s

Osiris

Asar, Ausir, Wesir, Osir

Khenti-Amentiu - Foremost of the Westerners
Un-Nofer - The Beatified (or Eternally Fresh)
Neb Abju - Lord of Abydos
Neb Djedu - Lord of Busiris

Scholars have debated the antiquity of Osiris' worship. He took on attributes of two local chthonic deities, Andjety of Busiris and Khentiamentiu of Abydos, but the earliest known references to Osiris Himself date from the Fifth Dynasty. To put that time into perspective, the Great Pyramids of Giza are older than our first texts mentioning Osiris.

Regardless of relative age, Osiris quickly established Himself as one of the most important and popular Gods of ancient Egypt, His annual Mysteries in Abydos becoming a major source of pilgrimage from the Middle Kingdom onward. The story of His demise, typically at the hands of His brother **Seth**, followed by His mummification by **Anubis** and resurrection by **Isis**, then His vindication by His son **Horus** became central motifs in Egyptian religion. One could argue that Egyptian children knew the story of Osiris as readily as children today would recognize the opening words, "A long time ago, in a galaxy far, far away".

His worship extended into Nubia from at least the New Kingdom, and statues of Him have been found in Nubian sites. But the practice of mummification never caught on in Nubian culture, so that aspect of Osiris' story had less significance for them.

Lords of the Underworld in some religions are frightening, vengeful beings. What makes Osiris different, and indeed what probably accounted for much of His popularity in ancient times, is His morality. He only need be feared by those who act wickedly in this life. As pharaoh of *Duat*, He does command an entire spirit world of threatening beings; in *The Contendings of Horus and Seth*, what finally settled Their rivalry was Osiris' reminder to the other Gods that everything must eventually die and enter His realm, where those Underworld spirits wait to devour the hearts of wrongdoers. But for the just, Osiris is a beneficent king who graciously welcomes them and provides them a place in the Fields of Peace.

Osiris also has relevance in the world of the living. Agriculture is one of His gifts to humankind. Because seeds must be buried to bring forth new life, Osiris is identified with the harvested crops, especially barley and emmer wheat. Pharaonic Egypt used a barter economy, and grain measures - Osiris' patron commodity - were one type of exchangeable unit. By extension into our modern world, this could put Him in charge of money and material wealth. How might He judge those who act greedily with His munificence?

Today, many Isians and Tameran Wiccans honor Osiris as their Lord to Isis' Lady. He also takes a prominent role in the Asar-Auset Society. Occasionally questions circulate the Internet about a supposed link between Osiris and Jesus (or else Horus and Jesus); rest assured that the only thing They have in common is that both were worshiped in Egypt at one time or another. Those conspiracy theories aside, Osiris would most certainly continue to preside over agriculture and food production - the staffs of life since civilization began. As Lord of Justice, or *ma'at*, He would an ideal intercessor for legal problems. He would certainly have a unique empathy for victims of violent crime.

In private observances, we have found Osiris to be calm, patient, almost soft-spoken. He sounds like someone who has all of eternity to work with, and thus has no need to hurry or fuss. Even His traditional Egyptian food taboos of fish and pork don't always bother Osiris; He would rather see to it that His followers enjoy a good meal than not eat, just to avoid having fish or pork in His presence. I can still recall one year when we planned to observe the Khoiakh, or Osiris Mysteries, but had to help our friend through a personal crisis at the last minute. So instead we actually ended up roasting pork ribs and bacon poppers on the back patio next to Osiris' altar - a feast for our 'baconphile' friend, but a nightmare of proscribed Osirian offerings! I asked Osiris to regard the pork as the hearts of His defeated enemies, which was traditionally done with other meat offerings. I got no sense whatsoever that He was offended. And while we didn't host an official ritual, our friend had his own 'rebirth' that weekend: it marked the beginning of his sobriety, now almost five years going. Osiris works in mysterious ways.

Offerings: Osiris has an affinity for myrrh, but especially for pine-scented or pine resin incense. (I would dare say that just pine trees in general have a strong connection with Him.) Wine and cool water make particularly appropriate libation offerings. Fresh vegetables, especially home-grown, honor His role in agriculture. Emmer wheat can be found packaged as pearled Italian Farro, which also makes a great offering. To that end, Pagan friends have come to know my "dirty Farro" dish (say it aloud and you get the joke) that combines cooked emmer wheat and ground meat. Often served for Kemetic holidays, it always gets eaten heartily, double entendres aside.

Feast Days: After the first national holiday of New Year's, Osiris claims the next one in the Wagy Feast, the first of three important festivals for the blessed dead. A "Going Forth" festival four days later may be connected to a wrap-up of the Wagy Feast. A week later in Abydos, He celebrated a general festival 'with His Ennead', which would include Isis and **Nephthys** as well as Horus. He is mourned in early October, then a few weeks later celebrates another feast in Abydos. But his holiday *par excellence* is the Khoiakh (derived from *Ka-Hor-Ka*)

Mysteries, which commemorated His death, recovery and embalming, then resurrection. It marked the second and largest festival of the dead in ancient Egypt, paralleling All Soul's Day or Dia de los Muertes today. In December at Abydos, another holiday marked the Raising of the *Djed* pillar, one of Osiris' symbols; this may have been a repetition of the *Djed*-raising as part of the Mysteries. In January He has a festival as Unnofer, which coincides with a feast of fellow chthonic deity Sokar. In spring, He is invoked as part of the harvest Feast of Min. At the start of the last month of the year He holds another festival as Unnofer, then a general celebration on the last day of the year. His birthday comes as the first of the five Epagomenal Days, or Days Upon the Year.

Great Hymn to Osiris

(from the Stela of Amunmose)

Inodj har-ek Osir, neb neheh, nisut notjeru,
Praise to You, Osiris, Lord of Eternity, King of the Gods,

asha' ranu, djoser khoperu, seshta iru im pir!
of many names, of holy forms, of secret rites in temples!

Shopses ka pu khenty Djadu, ur geret im Sakhem,
This noble *ka* at the fore of Djedu, great also in Sekhem,

neb hekenu im Andjety, khenty djefa im Iunu,
lord of praise in Andjety, foremost of offerings in Iunu,

neb sekhau im Ma'aty, ba seshta, neb kereret,
Lord of memory in *Ma'aty*, secret *ba*, lord of the cavern,

djoser im Ineb-hadj, ba Ra djet-ef djos-ef,
holy in White-Walls, *ba* of Ra of His very body,

hotep im Henes, monekh henu im narit,
at rest in Henes, excellent of praise in the *narit*-tree

khoper-es tjesit ba-ef. Neb hat a'ah im Khemnu,
that grew to raise His *ba*. Lord of the Great Shrine in Khemnu,

a'ah niru im Shas-hotep, neb neheh, khenty Abju
great of terror in Shas-hotep, Lord of Eternity, foremost of Abydos

hir wai sut-ef im Ta-Djoser.
in His distant place of the Sacred Land.

Djed ran in rou en romitju, Pauty en Tawy,
Name that endures in the mouths of people, Primeval One of the Two Lands,

Tum djefa kau khenty Paut Notjeru,
Nourisher at the fore of the Ennead of the Gods,

Akh menekh imim akhu pen.
Potent *akh* among the *akh*'s.

Rdi-en-ef Nun mu-ef, khenti-en-ef Mehyt,
Nun has given Him His waters,
the North Wind journeys to Him,

moses Resut er fened er-ef hotep-tu ib-ef.
Dusk brings the South Wind to His nose
to please His heart.

Neb hennu in pet Resyt, dua'u im pet Mehtet,
Lord of praise in the Southern sky,
praised in the Northern sky,

Iukhem-seku chir sut har-ef,
The Imperishable Stars are under His rule,

sut-ef pu Iukhem-seku.
[for] His abode is the Imperishable Stars.

Ptah

Titles:
Neb Ma'at - Lord of Ma'at
Sedjem Nehit - Hearer of Prayers
Nisut Tawy - King of the Two Lands
Neb Ineb-Hadj - Lord of White-Walls

A creator God, Ptah's center of worship lay in the capital city of Memphis. Ptah was patron of craftsmen and metalworkers (attributes He shared with **Sokar**), and He was credited with devising the Opening of the Mouth ritual to bring life to statues and the mummified bodies of the dead. He created the world by speaking names as His heart (seat of intelligence in Egyptian thought) prompted Him, thus bringing all things into being. In this respect, Ptah can be understood as embodying that point where creativity manifests in physical form, through drawing, sculpting, or building. Today as in ages past, Ptah would be the patron of artisans and craftspeople of all types, including cosplay builders and plushie artists.

Not surprisingly, residents of Deir el-Medina - home to the artisans responsible for the Valley of the Kings - revered Ptah. They honored Him during the Feast of Lifting the Sky, in which He took a role identified with **Shu**. Ptah formed a creation trinity with **Amun** and **Ra**, as well as an Underworld trinity with **Sokar** and **Osiris**. The fact that Ptah took part in both trinities indicated His key role in both creation and renewal. His wife is the Goddess **Sakhmet** (occasionally **Bastet**), and Their son is **Nefertum** or **Khonsu**. The famed vizier and sage Imhotep, architect of the Step Pyramid, was later deified as another son of Ptah and Sakhmet.

In our world, prototypes of all kinds could come under Ptah's patronage. Toys and action figures, seen as frivolous by many but which hearken back to the ritual figurines of ancient times, would also fall within Ptah's domain. Ptah also seems to have a sense of humor. While standing in front of Ptah's gilded statue from the tomb of Tutankhamun during an exhibit, my husband quipped, "And the Oscar goes to...!" Could filmmaking be another part of Ptah's patronage, and humor was His way of telling us this?

Offerings: Traditional offerings of water, beer, wine, fruits and breads work well for Ptah, as do frankincense and sandalwood incenses. Silver is also cited as an offering, perhaps as part of His connection to Sokar. In His triple aspect with Sokar and Osiris, myrrh and conifer incenses, as well as onions, would be appropriate.

Feast Days: Had more survived from His ancient temple of Memphis, we would probably have an extensive calendar for Ptah. New Year's would surely have been its big 'kickoff', followed by a Feast of Drunkenness for His wife Sakhmet. We do have documentation for more than one holiday of Ptah Lifting the Sky, however. The first comes in December, on the first of *Makhir*; then another in January one month later that was observed in Esna temple. At the last two days of the year, He celebrated a 'Feast of Sokar in the House of Ptah' followed by year-end festivities. Based on what we know of other temple calendars, a safe conjecture would be that He held major festivals at the start of each season (see the next chapter for a fuller discussion), a procession or festival in connection with the Sokar Festival and Osiris Mysteries, then a festival for His son Nefertum during the harvest season.

Creation Litany to Ptah

(from the Shabaka Stone)

Eyes seeing, ears hearing, noses breathing,
All these report to the heart;
It makes all understanding come forth.
Tongue repeats what heart has devised.

Thus were all the gods born,
Atum and his Ennead,
For every word of the god comes about
Through what the heart plans
And the tongue commands.

Thus was Ptah satisfied
After making all things and sacred words.

He gave birth to the gods,
He made Their villages,
He founded Their estates,
Set Them in Their temples,
Ensured Their offerings,
Founded Their shrines,
Made Their bodies as They wished.

Thus the gods entered Their bodies,
Of every wood, stone, and clay,
All things that grow upon Him,
In which They came to be.

Thus were gathered unto Him
All the gods and Their *ka*s,
Contented and united
With the Lord of the Two Lands.

Ra
Re, Pre

Titles:
Neb Pesdjet - Lord of the Nine
Wa en Nun - Sole One of Nun
Neb-er-Djer - Lord to the Limit
Hor-Akhety - Horus of the Horizon

As Khopri:
Notjer a'ah - Greatest God
Ka mut-ef - Bull of His Mother
Djoser-remen - Sweeping shoulder
Nub hekenu - Gold of jubilation

As Atum:
Imy-Nun - He Who Is In Nun
Neheh - Eternal (Or Eternally Renewing)
Neb Neheh - Lord of Eternity
Nedj-der-ef - Limitless One

Worship of Ra first came to prominence during the Archaic Period. Scholars consider the Old Kingdom to be Ra's heyday, when kings first adopted the title 'Son of Ra' and the Fifth Dynasty rulers built sun temples at Abusir. Ra's primary center of worship was Iunu, called 'Heliopolis' by the Greeks. Like a mystery fit for Indiana Jones, in pharaonic times Heliopolis was a sprawling temple complex whose priesthood gained renown for their sacred libraries and learning; but today the site is something of a 'lost city' buried beneath the north Cairo suburb of Matariya, whose remains turn up in tantalizing fragments that suggest Ra's 'heyday' might have lasted longer than we currently know.

Early on, Ra absorbed Atum, the creator whose name means 'completed one' or 'perfected one'. Atum appears in art as a man, sometimes an old man, wearing the double crown. As Ra-Atum He created the Ennead, or group of nine Gods, of Heliopolis. In the Old Kingdom Ra took on attributes of Elder **Horus**, including the appellation *Horakhety*, 'Horus of the Twin Horizons'. Ra's other major aspect - in the *Litany of Ra*, He is credited with seventy-five different manifestations - is Khopri, the scarab beetle. In the Egyptian language, the scarab sign spells the word *kheper*, which means 'to become', 'to exist', or 'change'. Khopri's name has been rendered as the 'Evolver'; dare we add, the 'Transformer'. As a triad of forms, Khopri represents the newborn sun at dawn. Ra-Horakhety as a hawk-headed man represents noon, while at sundown He is identified as Atum. This was probably the origin of the Greeks' riddle of the Sphinx: *What has four legs at morning* (Khopri as the sun-child), *two legs at high noon* (Ra), *and three legs at evening* (Atum)?

Today Ra continues to make cameos in pop culture. Aside from being cast as the villain(!?!) in *Stargate* and having perhaps one of the least objectionable portrayals in *Gods of Egypt* (which is almost universally panned by Egyptian Pagans), Ra appears as a humorous mascot in commercials for Solar City and Sun Butter. His symbols can be encountered in seemingly mundane settings, such the Mexican sun faces, which blend European and Aztec solar symbols. My husband has even described being visited by Ra in the form of the Raisin Bran mascot, complete with scoops of raisins in hand!

The ancients revered Ra as King of the Gods, and even today He possesses the bearing of a leader more than that of a close companion. Some deities have been described by Their followers as friendly and personable; by contrast, Egyptian Pagans who've worked with Ra report that He does not get "chummy" with them. He is still fair-minded (as Lord of *ma'at*, He is at times painfully fair), concerned and even compassionate, but He holds His followers to a higher standard. Ellen Cannon

Reed, author of *Circle of Isis*, related an encounter with Ra where He was most displeased about an injustice that had been done - but also upset that she didn't seek His aid first. Given that ancient Egyptian texts contain references to ordinary people praying to Ra and telling Him their problems at sunrise, He probably wanted her to ask Him for help in the traditional manner. As a priestess of the Notjeru (as His reasoning probably went), why shouldn't she?

Despite this, Ra does have some sense of humor; but He seems to share it most with those who are not His followers, such as average non-Pagan viewers of solar panel commercials, or my non-Pagan husband whenever we venture out on a sunny day and he forgets to use the sun shade. (He said he often hears, "Hey, buddy, how are ya?!" as he squints in the bright sunlight and reaches for the car visor.) As my husband summarized Ra's *modus operandi* with those He considers His own, "Parenting is serious business."

Offerings: Frankincense, myrrh and kyphi (Egyptian *kapet*), a special type of moist incense blend unique to ancient Egyptian tradition, are Ra's signature incenses. Copal resin, which has solar associations, is especially appropriate for occasions such as New Year's. Cinnamon - whether in incense, fragrant oils or as a spice - also has a strong connection with Ra. Traditional offerings of bread, fruit, cool water, wine and beer are appreciated, though Ra is also reported to enjoy occasional sweets. That said, if you shouldn't be eating sweets, He will insist on healthier offerings - it's for your own good, you know.

Feast Days: Egyptian New Year's centers very much on Ra. It celebrates His birth at the beginning of time, or *Zep Tepy* (the 'First Time'). Three weeks into the year He celebrates a Purification (presumably involving lustrations of water and censing). In October, a holiday honors **Ma'at** being raised to Ra.

In mid-October He has a feast of rejoicing, then another raising of Ma'at in December. The date of *Makhir* 30, in January in modern usage, marked the mid-point of the year and another special observance referred to in the Book of the Dead as 'Filling the Sacred Eye'. In the Kemetic Reform tradition, this is honored as a sacred time to Ra and His Eye.

Ra and His Eye celebrate another holiday one month later - which seems to fit a broader pattern of key festivals in a particular month being celebrated alternately on the first or last day, depending on location. In Iunu, Ra-Horakhety had a Sailing festival in early March, near the start of the harvest season. He is involved in a feast with Neith in late May, and several of the feasts of Khnum in this season connect to Ra as well. As was the case for other major deities, Ra probably had a feast on the last day of the year. As with Ptah, we can only hypothesize about what themes and dates that a full festival calendar for Iunu would have contained.

The following is an excerpt from Chapter 17 of the Book of the Dead, which itself is 'descended' from Coffin Text 335. Evidently a popular hymn to Ra as the Creator, in the Book of the Dead it contains the instruction, "As for anyone who shall read it daily for their own benefit, it means being well on earth."

Daily Praises and Recitations of Ra

*(From Spell 335 of the Coffin Texts,
Chapter 17 of the Book of the Dead)*

Khoperu djedut nibet Neb-er-Djer:
Now come to be all the words of the Lord of All:

Inuk Atum im unin wa ku-i; khoper-en-i im Nun.
I am Atum when I was alone; I came into being in Nun.

Inuk Ra im khay-ef, im sha'a heqa ir-en-ef.
I am Ra in His rising, in the beginning ruling that which He has made.

Inuk notjer a'ah khoper djosef,
I am the Great God who came into being Himself,

mu pu, Nun pu, it-en Notjeru.
the waters, Nun, the Father of the Gods.

Pu-teri iref-su?
What does it mean?

Ra pu qema'im ran-en atu-ef;
It is Ra, who created the names of His limbs;

khoper-en-en pu im Notjeru imiu nakht Ra.
They have come into being as the Gods in Ra's suite.

Inuk nety khes-ef im Notjeru.
I am unopposed among the gods.

Inuk saf, rekh-ku-i dua'u.
I am Yesterday, I know Tomorrow.

Pu-teri iref-su?
What does it mean?

Ir saf Osir pu, ir dua'u Ra pu,
Yesterday is Osiris, tomorrow is Ra,

Heru pui en sehetim khaftiu-ef en Neb-er-djer
On that day of destroying the wicked foes of the Lord of All

hena seheqa-tu sa-ef Horu;
and of crowning His son Horus.

Ir-en-i aha' Notjeru kheft udjat-ef Osir neb Dju Amentet.
I made the battleground of the Gods as Osiris, Lord of the Western Desert, commanded.

Iu-i rekh-ku-i Notjer pui a'ah nety im-es.
I know the Great God who is in it.

Inuk Bennu pui a'ah nety im Iunu.
I am the Great Phoenix who is in Iunu.

Inuk iry sipu en nety unen.
I am the Overseer that which exists.

Pu-teri iref-su?
What does it mean?

Osir pu; key djed, ir sipu nety unen khat-ef pu.
It is Osiris; otherwise said, that which exists is his body.

Key djed, en ir neheh pu hena djed;
Otherwise said, it is Eternal Renewal and Everlastingness;

Ir neheh pu heru, ir djet pu gereh.
Eternal Renewal is the day, Everlastingness is night.

Inuk Min im Poret-ef
I am Min in His Going Forth;

Iu rdi-en-i Shuty im tep-i.
I have placed the Dual Plumes on my head.

Inuk Miu pui a'ah nety pesesh Ished ir-ges-ef im Iunu
I am the Great Cat who split the Ished on its side in Iunu

Gereh pui en aha-a,
on that night of war,

Irit sau sebiu heru pui en hetem khaftiu en Neb-er-Djer im-ef.
Of warding off the rebels on that day on which
were destroyed the wicked foes of the Lord of All.

Pu-teri iref-su?
What does it mean?

Ir Miu pui a'ah nety pesesh Ished ir-ges-ef im Iunu
That Great Cat who split the Ished on its side in Iunu

Ra pu djos-ef, djed-tu miu er-ef im djed Sia
It is Ra Himself, called "Cat" when Sia said of Him,

mi su im nan ir-en-ef, khoper ran-ef im Miu.
"How like Him, by what He has done," and
His name became Cat.

Iwau kheser, sek djuu.
Wrongdoing is overthrown, evil is destroyed.

Ma'a-en-i Ra mosu im sef er khepdet en Mehet-Uret;
I have seen Ra born of the hind-quarters of the Great Flood;

udjai-ef udjai-i, tjis rer.
If He is well, then I am well, and vice versa.

Sakhmet

Sachmis, Sekhmet

Titles:
Irit (en) Ra - Eye of Ra
Nebet Senedjet - Mistress of Fear
Khenti Per-Neser - Foremost of the House of Flame
Nebet Tawy - Mistress of the Two Lands

Sakhmet, the "Powerful One", is both daughter of **Ra** and His Eye, and wife of **Ptah**, thus mother to **Nefertum** or **Khonsu, Horus** in certain local aspects, and later in Egyptian history the deified form of the vizier Imhotep. Sakhmet combines the seemingly opposite forces of implacable divine fury and healing, nurturing divine grace. Humans both ancient and modern have sought to explain how these forces juxtapose. In the *Myth of Destruction of Mankind*, Ra sends Sakhmet in the form of a lioness to destroy rebellious humans; She gets so swept up in Her wholesale slaughter that it quickly becomes apparent to Ra that She will leave no humans alive to serve the Gods. The Gods then trick Sakhmet into drinking a lake of beer colored red to resemble blood, and she passes out drunk (hence the multiple "Feasts of Drunkenness" in the Egyptian calendar). As the *Myth of Destruction*, in the form known from New Kingdom pharaohs' tombs, explains it, Sakhmet wakes up and changes into **Hathor**, the 'Beautiful One'. It's possible that variations of this story gave rise to later connections between Sakhmet as a vengeful aspect and **Bastet** as a friendly aspect of the same feline Goddess, known especially from the Late and Greco-Roman Periods.

Even today, Sakhmet's dual nature challenges understanding. A mainstream Pagan acquaintance once told me, upon seeing my icon of Sakhmet, that someone gave her a book about Sakhmet with the note, 'Do not invoke except in extreme emergencies!'. (I never found out what book it was, but from this fellow Pagan's description, it cast Sakhmet as a dangerously powerful and unpredictable entity.) Goddesses of both love *and* war, which are common in ancient Middle Eastern religions, contrast sharply with the prevailing modern vision of the Mother Goddess. Sakhmet confronts the notion of deities as simple archetypes, because Her nature *is* complex. She can both kill and heal. Scholastic works describe Her as manifesting the sun's destructive heat; but every time I have stood in front of one of Her statues in a museum, I always felt a cool breath of air. My husband, who has a disability, has also noticed his joint pain go away in Her presence. The best way to sum up these two sides of Sakhmet, the Powerful One, is with the old wisdom, "It takes strength to be gentle."

Some mainstream Pagans recognize Her complex nature, and in fact Sakhmet has a modern temple dedicated to Her in Cactus Springs, Nevada. A few years ago, the temple's statue of Sakhmet was stolen and had to be replaced - but reportedly the group of teenagers responsible confessed to their crime and apologized. No telling what retribution the Eye of Ra visited upon them!

Because Her ancient priests practiced as doctors and surgeons, those professions would still fall under Her purview today. As mistress of both war and healing, Sakhmet would be the ideal patroness of EMT's, paramedics and army surgeons, as well as women serving in the military or law enforcement. Physical therapy and rehab, which can often be painful but are necessary for healing, could be considered Her work. And of course, She is a loving and nurturing patroness to many Kemetics. Even non-Pagans receive Her blessings - as long as they act in accord with *ma'at*.

Offerings: Sakhmet has strong solar associations. Frankincense, sandalwood and cinnamon incenses all work well for Her, as can copal. Beer is certainly a favorite, even when not stained red. In lieu of alcoholic offerings, pomegranate juice is reportedly well-received. She has an affinity for savory foods, especially those seasoned with cinnamon and 'solar' herbs such as rosemary.

Feast Days: During the Days Upon the Year and going through New Year's, litanies were chanted to Sakhmet to seek good fortune and protection from Her 'Arrows'. Three weeks later, Her sparing of humanity was celebrated in the Feast of *Tekhy*. She had a feast in Esna at the beginning of the month of *Hat-Hor*, then a shared festival with Bastet in late October. At Edfu, the "Appeasing Sakhmet" litanies were chanted again during the Coronation of the Sacred Falcon, and She seems to have had a role in the national Feast of Neheb-kau as well. She has feasts again in December (perhaps playing a role in the Establishing of the Celestial Cow), and as the Eye of Ra could be invoked at the winter Feast of Filling the Sacred Eye. In a regional feast dating from the Middle Kingdom She shared a festival with Horus of Sepa, honored as Her son, at the start of the harvest season. Sakhmet received a Purification in Esna in late April; a feast of "Eating Cucumbers by the Eye of Horus" at Edfu during late May or mid-June has been interpreted by some as a festival of Sakhmet, but see the discussion under "Observances Then and Now" next chapter. And of course, as the calendar draws to a close, Sakhmet is again invoked to bring a safe and prosperous new year.

The text on the following page is a specific adaptation of the Litany of the Seven Arrows from Edfu, which originally did not assign any properties or names to the Arrows. It has become a part of our New Year's tradition, often recited over a bonfire with sistrums rung in accompaniment.

Litany to Sakhmet and the Seven Arrows

1) Hail, Sakhmet, Who presides over the land, Lady of Flourishing, Generous One, Sakhmet who protects the Two Lands! Come to us who are under Your sway! Save us, protect us, and preserve us from the First Arrow of Famine!

2) Hail, Sakhmet, oh Curl, oh Hidden Lady, Wadjit the Great! Come to us who are under Your sway! Save us, protect us, and preserve us from the Second Arrow of Drought!

3) Hail, Sakhmet, who moves in light, who terrifies the gods with Her massacre! Come to us who are under Your sway! Save us, protect us, and preserve us from the Third Arrow of War!

4) Hail, Sakhmet, who guides mankind, Lady of the Dual Shores, Mistress of humanity! Come to us who are under Your sway! Save us, protect us, and preserve us from the Fourth Arrow of Terror!

5) Hail, Sakhmet, Great Shining One, Foremost in the Mansion of Flame *(Per Neser)*, Who terrorizes the Two Lands with fear! Come to us who are under Your sway! Save us, protect us, and preserve us from the Fifth Arrow of Storms!

6) Hail, Sakhmet, who loves Ma'at and hates *isfet*, Lady of the people! Come to us who are under Your sway! Save us, protect us, and preserve us from the Sixth Arrow of Oppression!

7) Hail, Sakhmet, Uraeus who opens the acacia, Great and Sovereign One! Come to us who are under Your sway! Save us, protect us, and preserve us from the Seventh Arrow of Disease!

Serqet

Serket is a goddess of healing and protection, especially through magickal means. In both spells to protect a bedroom and in funerary materials, She stands guard as one of the "Four Noble Ladies" alongside **Isis**, **Nephthys** and **Neith**. She also protects nursing mothers and children, especially against snakes and scorpions, the latter serving as Her emblem. In the *Duat*, or Underworld, she casts nets together with Isis in order to entrap the evil serpent A'apep and prevent him from attacking **Ra**'s sun barge during its nightly journey.

Serket's name comes from the Egyptian word for "breathe". Her full title is *Serket hetyt*, meaning, "She makes throats breathe". Due to these unique traits, she could be regarded as a helper to asthmatics and those with respiratory ailments. Because of her ability to cure poisons, the Kemetic Orthodox looks to Serket as a healer of addictions; but this view misinterprets the causes of *addiction*, which is not the same as *chemical dependence*. Serket's patron professions would include respiratory therapy and poison control.

Offerings: The traditional water, bread, fruit and vegetable offerings work well for Serket. Healing herbs have also been offered to Her. In this vein, soothing and medicinal foods (seasoned with those beneficial herbs - think turmeric, coriander or ginger) would make excellent choices. Sandalwood, frankincense and ginger incenses are also good choices for Serket.

Feast Days: No specific feast days for Serket are known at present. As with other deities, Her important holidays would probably include New Year's, the beginning of Poret (winter) and

Shomu (harvest) seasons, and the end of the year. She may have also played a role in the Feast of Neheb-kau, having a connection to the chthonic serpent deity Neheb-kau.

Prayer-Hymn to Serket

(adapted from her titles in the Pyramid and Coffin Texts)

Hail, oh Serket, oh Noble Lady,
Serket-Hetyt, Giver of breath!
Come unto me, oh Lady of Heaven,
Drive out every evil that is in my body.
With Your fire in Your mouth and Your flame before you,
Set Your spells against all those who wish me ill!
Mistress of Your Mansion among the Undying Stars,
Mistress of the Cavern, Who protects the Barque of Ra!

Seshat

Sefkhet-Abwy

The 'lady scribe', Seshat presided over astronomy, mathematics and architecture. She was invoked at the founding ceremonies for new temples, said to record the years of a king's reign and his deeds in battle. Her leopard-hide vestment symbolized Her stewardship of arcane knowledge. She could work in tandem with **Djehuty**, either as His consort or His professional partner.

That the ancient Egyptians worshiped a Goddess of record-keeping and sciences while mortal women in their society seldom received a formal education is certainly ironic to our twenty-first century sensibilities. Unfortunately, that dichotomy is not unique to ancient Egypt. Studies of modern Hinduism reveal the same attitude, still alive and well, that probably kept girls from entering temples to study under Seshat's tutelage: that Goddesses are different, better, and more deserving of respect than ordinary women, so therefore a double standard is okay. (The quote from a Hindu man given in *Women and Goddess Traditions* is shockingly more frank.) This scholarship not only proves that simply having Goddesses to worship doesn't automatically make a culture more gender-equal, but it also gives us modern Pagans much food for thought, especially when we consider Goddesses like Seshat.

Without question, today Seshat would be the patroness *par excellence* of women in STEM (science, technology, engineering and mathematics) fields as either students or professionals. Female authors, astrologers and priestesses would also come under Her purview; keep in mind that the ancients considered science to be an extension of magick and sacred scriptures. Of course, men working in these fields could still look to Seshat's guidance. They just no longer have an exclusive audience with Her.

Offerings: Seshat is sometimes given similar offerings to Djehuty because of Their close association. One certainly can't go wrong with traditional Egyptian staples of cool water, bread and fruit, or sandalwood incense. Symbolically offering Her writing or study projects, and the effort involved to make them, would be another excellent way to honor Seshat.

Feast Days: As with Serket, no major feasts in honor of Seshat are known. She could share observances with Djehuty, and would surely be feted at the turn of the seasons and the year.

Much like Nut, texts mentioning Seshat prove too incomplete to yield a full hymn. The archana-style chant given here includes known titles, and feminized forms of titles She would share with Her colleague Djehuty.

Chant For Seshat

Dua Seshat, seshat notjery
Adoration to Seshat, holy female scribe

Dua Seshat, Sefkhet Abwy
Adoration to Seshat, the Seven-Pointed One

Dua Seshat, ikeret en saret
Adoration to Seshat, excelling in wisdom

Dua Seshat, nebet medu notjer
Adoration to Seshat, Mistress of the sacred words

Dua Seshat, nebet ma'at
Adoration to Seshat, Lady of *ma'at*

Dua Seshat, notjerit a'aht
Adoration to Seshat, Great Goddess

Seth

Set, Setesh, Sutekh

Titles:
Neb Nubet - Lord of Gold-Town (Ombos)
Neb Deshret - Lord of the Desert
A'ah Pehty - Greatest of Strength
Sa Nut - Son of Nut

Seth, sometimes referred to as Sutekh or Setesh, is a complicated deity. Some Pagans avoid Seth and His worship entirely, owing to His dangerous aspects as the murderer of **Osiris** and usurper of natural order. Still other Pagans, especially followers of the Left-Hand Path, have adopted Seth as their patron precisely because of His 'evil' - or at least, contrarian - reputation. (His adherents are often quick to point out versions of the Osirian legend where Osiris simply drowned, with no explicit reference to fratricide.) Seth is the Lord of the barren desert, of storms, chaotic disruption and exotic foreignness. His character has been the subject of numerous online disputes among Kemetics; which in itself is probably truer to Seth's nature than anything actually said within those debates.

Modern devotees describe Seth as a rather strict patron, embodying 'tough love' and the confronting of personal issues and illusions. He has also been described as somewhat militaristic in character - perhaps making Seth another candidate for patronage of servicemen and -women, or even of drill instructors. But another possible, and highly overlooked, role stems from Seth's ancient reputation as Lord of wastelands and antithesis of fertility. As "closer of the womb", Seth could act as an ideal helper to women who do not wish to have children and a patron of contraception in general. Appropriate to Seth's controversial nature, this patronage could be logically extended to abortion as well.

One last point about Seth deserves mention here. The prevailing view of Seth's history is that His worship decreased in the Late Period and afterward, as He became more closely identified with foreign and demonic forces. The Kemetic Reconstructionist book Eternal Egypt takes this originally academic view even further, declaring that it "resulted in a fatal impoverishment of the original Kemetic vision." But we have record of Seth's worship continuing in Dakhla Oasis and in rural villages well into the first centuries C.E., where He was identified with the Greek deity Typhon. In fact, our hymn to Seth given here draws in part from a Greco-Roman era document known as the London-Leiden Papyrus. Here Seth reminds us not to cling to initial assumptions too closely, no matter where they might have come from.

Offerings: Historically, Set favors Romaine lettuce and pork. Adherents also report His affinity for red foods, particularly strawberries and watermelon (the latter another historical association). Heavy flavors of incense, including dragon's blood, are also appropriate. He also favors hard liquors and foreign foods.

Feast Days: Festivals that *honor* Seth, as opposed to *execrating* Him, are not common in our surviving records but we do have a scant few. On the fourteenth of *Makhir*, or very late December, the Cairo Calendar gives a date where Seth kills 'the rebel'. However, their forecast advises people not to go out that day, so it may have been a less-than-festive day. He did have a full-on festival in June, however, and His birthday is observed during the Days Upon the Year - though again, that date was often considered unlucky in ancient times.

Hymn to Set

*(adapted from Ramesside titles and
the London-Leiden Papyrus)*

Hail, oh Sutekh, Son of Nut,
Great of Strength in the Bark of Millions!
Chosen One of Ra-Horakhety,
Bull who dwells in the northern sky!

Fearsome One, at Whom all lands tremble,
Great is your war-cry, great is Your might!
Your *Was*-scepter stretches over the sky,
You stand at the zenith of the stars!

Lord of storms, Lord of dread,
Your voice is thunder in the heavens!
You slay the Fiend from the prow of Ra's bark;
Protect us from evil and grant us long life!

Shu
Shou

Notjer a'ah - Greatest God
Neb ankh - Lord of Life
Irpat en Pesdjet - Prince of the Ennead

Often described as the 'god of air', or more descriptively as the 'god of sunlit air', Shu and His twin sister **Tefnut** were the first gendered pair created by **Atum** (see **Ra**), or in other accounts by **Neith** or **Ptah**. In art, Shu is pictured with arms upraised, holding his daughter **Nut** aloft; the Feast of Lifting the Sky commemorates how this act completed creation. (In some versions of the festival, Shu is identified with Ptah.) As the crown prince of Ra's Ennead, or group of nine Gods and Goddesses, Shu defends His father from the forces of evil, in which role He can combine with the elder aspect of **Horus** or the hunter **Inhur**.

His nature is described at its most profound and explicit in a series of spells from the Coffin Texts known as the Litany of Shu. He announces the will of His creator - perhaps anticipating the Kabbalistic figure of Metatron - and He represents cyclical, or *neheh*, time while His sister Tefnut embodies linear (*djet*) time. But most importantly, Shu is the breath of life itself. He is everywhere around us and yet unseen. One Kemetic described a visit to the desert, during which she felt she could finally 'get' Shu. Personally, I can relate a particularly intense attack that came on during a respiratory infection; at the precise moment I could finally draw in a lungful of air again, I heard the words, "*I am Shu. I am the breath of life.*" It was an intense, vivid revelation.

As the one who creates storm clouds and the colors of sunset, today Shu would be the patron of meteorologists - and potentially of storm chasers, though such derring-do might equally fall under the tutelage of **Seth**. But as the Breath of Life, Shu is the protector of those in respiratory distress. He would share tutelage with **Serket** over respiratory therapists and pulmonary specialists. By extension, rescue breathing - a component of CPR - can be viewed as a life-giving extension of Shu's work.

Offerings: Think "light and airy" with gifts to Shu; light incense fragrances (such as sandalwood or copal), mildly savory foods, herbs or plants associated with the element of air.

Feast Days: After the usual New Year's celebrations, Shu has a feast as 'Son of Ra' during the month of *Hat-Hor*. During the month of *Ta'Ibet*, He has a Going Forth, then another feast a few weeks later. He plays an important role in the various Lifting the Sky feasts, either as Himself or combined with Ptah. In May, He has a Going Forth that commemorates his role (as Inhur-Shu) in bringing back Tefnut. During the Appearance of Khnum not long after, Shu defends His father (as Khnum-Ra) against forces of evil.

The Litany of Shu

(From Coffin Texts 75 and 80)

I am He who foretells Ra when He
ascends from the *akhet*.
I put the fear of Him into whomever
seeks out His name.
I am the one among the *Heh*-Gods
who hears Their words;
I dispatch the word of the Self-Created
to the multitudes;
I am the one Who captains the
Sun-bark and its crew;

I am stronger and more raging
than all the Enneads.
I show splendor in accordance with My nature,
I speak and the Enneads are silent.
I am He whose shape was exhaled,
Whom this august God created,
Who strews the sky with His beauty,
Whose name the Gods do not know,
The One whom the sun-folk serve.

(the Litany continues:)
Shu is the one whom Atum fashioned,
His robe is the air of life.
A cry for Him went forth from the mouth of Atum,
The air opened upon His ways.
He makes the sky light after darkness,
His pleasing color is the breath of Atum.
Storm clouds in the sky are His efflux,
Hailstorms and dusk are His sweat.
The length of the sky is His stride,
The width of the earth are His settlements.
All living things upon the back of Geb,
By Atum's command does Shu govern them;
His life is in their nostrils,
He guides breath into their throats.

Sobek
Sebek, Suchos

Fearsome son of the equally formidable Goddess **Neith**, Sobek takes the form of a robust man with the head of a crocodile, or as a full-bodied crocodile. Interestingly, for centuries His animal form was identified as the Nile crocodile (*Crocodilus nilotica*); but DNA studies conducted in the 2000's identified a different species, the West African crocodile (*C. suchus*), to which all of the mummified crocodiles found in Egypt properly belong. The West African crocodile is smaller and more docile than the Nile crocodile, which would explain how ancient priests were able to successfully keep them in captivity (without ending up as Sobek's dinner!).

Like His animal avatar, Sobek seemed to possess a somewhat ambivalent nature. His strength, virility and terrifying power were universally revered, but hymns described Him as "He who loves taking" and even "Lord of plunder". Sporadic references in the Coffin Texts suggest that Sobek ate part of **Osiris**, and the Cairo Calendar mentions a date when Sobek's tongue was cut out. But other legends tell of Sobek inventing fishing nets to help **Horus**, (which may relate to His patronage of fishermen), and at the temple in Kom Ombo Sobek and Horus were worshiped side by side. There, Sobek took the place of **Seth** in the traditional duality with Horus. The 'Twin Crocodiles' birthed and nursed by Neith can thus be viewed as Horus and Sobek, or else Sobek and another solar deity: from the Middle Kingdom onward, Sobek became identified with **Ra**, forming the composite Sobek-Ra.

Today, Sobek is greatly revered by individual Kemetics for His power, strength and wisdom, just as He was in ancient times. As Lord of the Waters, His modern patronage could extend to fishing, water quality, hydraulics or hydroelectric power. Reptile enthusiasts, even those who don't consider themselves

Egyptian Pagan, have been known to express interest in Sobek; perhaps He might patronize herpetologists who specialize in crocodilians. In the American South, those would include the ubiquitous alligator (*Alligator mississipiensis*). Perhaps that reptilian connection inspired another blending of Old and New Worlds; today an American Mardi Gras organization calls itself the Krewe of Sobek.

Offerings: Sobek is reported to like beef and lamb, pita bread or crackers, wine and beer - a healthy appetite befitting His crocodile form. Frankincense, myrrh and rose-scented incenses seem to be preferred. His followers also offer to Him their personal efforts of learning, discipline and self-betterment.

Feast days: Roughly one month after the obligatory New Year's, Sobek of Ombos (Kom Ombo) celebrates His first specific festival. In October He may have been invoked in a feast to Hathor of Ombos, but has a holiday of conducting rites to Himself shortly afterward. He shares a Going Forth with Neith in late December - coinciding with Christmas on the Kemetic Reform calendar. (Pagans intent on spoofing Christmas themes with Egyptian deities are encouraged to look up *Gaston the Green-Nosed Alligator* by James Rice for an amusing parallel.) In March, Sobek has an Appearance Feast in Ombos, and may have been invoked during the Feast of Neith Saving Ra. Interestingly, the Cairo Calendar lists several days that were negative for Sobek. During those dates, (specifically *Djehutet* 17, *Pa'en-Opet* 22, *Pa'en-Rennutet* 25, and possibly *Pa-Khonsu* 14,) the typical advice was to eat no fish. Those wishing to express solidarity with Sobek can choose to abstain from fish or seafood on those days.

Hymn to Sobek

Hail to You, Twin of Ra,
Who arose from the Primeval Waters,
Lord of Ta-She, Son of Neith,
Mighty God whose seizing cannot be seen,
Ruler of the rivers, Governor of the winds,
Great Male, Rutting Bull, Lord of love,
Lord of *akhu* [spirits],
He who loves taking, Great of terror!
Drive off Your wrath, Let pass your raging,
Cut short Your mourning,
Let Your beauty come,
Welcome in peace,
Lord of peace!
- *adapted from Ramesseum Papyrus VI*

Another Hymn to Sobek

Hail, oh Sobek, Great God, Lord of
Ta-She [Lake Land],
Great Male who came from Nun,
White of teeth, green of scales,
Keen of face and raised of brow,
Lord of strength and virility,
Raging One who drives away evil!
You are Lord of the Nile who makes
the Two Banks green [flourish],
Lord of the Winding Waterway in the sky,
In Your carnelian temple in the mountain of Bakhu!
-*adapted from titles of Sobek*

Sokar
Seker, Soker, Sokaris

Titles:
Neb Rosetau - Lord of Rosetau
Heqa Iugaret - Ruler of the Silent Land
Neb Kereret - Lord of the Cavern
Neb Neheh - Lord of Eternal Renewal (cyclical time)

An ancient deity hailing from the region of Memphis, Sokar presides over caverns and underground realms, cemeteries and the Underworld. The site known today as Saqqara echoes His name. In this role, He appears as a falcon-headed man. But early on, Sokar began combining aspects with **Ptah,** the creator in Memphite tradition, to form Ptah-Sokar. This may have been inspired by a shared association with craftsmen and metallurgy; silver is particularly associated with Sokar. But as Lord of the Dead, Sokar went on to combine with **Osiris** as Osiris-Sokar. Eventually the three deities merged into a trinity, Ptah-Sokar-Osiris, who took the form of a mummiform man crowned with ram's horns, a sun disc and twin feathers. This triune form sometimes confuses modern Pagans, much as the Amun-Ra-Ptah trinity does. But just as Amun-Ra-Ptah manifests different, distinct aspects of the original Creator, Ptah-Sokar-Osiris represents distinct aspects of life, death, and renewal manifested in a complex God.

In a local Pagan group, we hosted a Feast of Sokar one year in order to include an Isian friend who had been dedicated to **Seth** and thus had to abstain from the Osiris Mysteries (not a very Seth-friendly liturgy). This could have broader application for other Sethian Pagans. In our group, we found Sokar to be quiet and sparse with words, but patient. His patron professions could include welding and metal-working. In ancient times, it was considered proper to honor Sokar before doing any digging or excavation work; in that regard, our modern society is rather behind on its respects. As sinkholes become a more frequent urban phenomenon, perhaps we should consider acknowledging the Lord of Caverns before tunneling in His domain.

Offerings: Silver and silver-colored items are associated with Sokar. Food offerings include green onions, wine, dates and sweet spices. Myrrh and conifer incenses (cedar, juniper, etc.) seem to work best for Him.

Feast Days: If identified with Osiris, Sokar's first observance of the year would be at the Wagy Feast. He figures prominently in the Osiris (Khoiakh) Mysteries; the day of His feast historically involved circling the walls of Memphis or other temple enclosures in His distinctive gazelle-head ornamented *Henu* barque, with a host of Goddesses and Gods in tow. In early January, He celebrated another festival at Ro-setau, the cemetary outside Memphis. He held a final feast of the year in the 'House of Ptah' shortly before the year's end.

Hymn to Sokar
Going-Around-the-Walls
(adapted from Papyrus Bremner-Rhind)

Hail, Sokar, lord of Ro-setau!
Hail, oh golden remedy!
Hail, Sokar, keeper of caverns!
Hail, Lord of eternity!

Sokar, take hold of Your shrine!
Sokar, take hold of Your temple!
Sokar, take hold of Your offerings!
Sokar, take hold of Your city!

Sokar is crowned, Lord of the Feast!
Sokar is crowned, Lord of the Feast!

Tawret

Tauret, Taweret, Thoeris

Titles:
Uret hekau - Great of Magic

Tawret's image can seem even more confusing than Her name, which is perhaps best pronounced 't-OW-ret'. Portrayed as a composite being with a lion's legs, hippo's head, crocodile's tail and the distended belly and breasts of a pregnant woman, Tawret had no dedicated temples, but probably all ancient Egyptians knew Her. A domestic goddess who protected pregnant and nursing women and young children, Her form was carved into wands and magickal amulets and ceramic vases meant to hold breast milk. A monumental statue of Queen Tiye, wife of Amunhotep III, in the guise of Tawret probably received much supplication from ordinary Egyptians looking to protect and grow their families. Tawret may be one and the same Goddess as Ipy, Apip or Opet (the latter having a shrine built to Her in Karnak during the Late Period). In which case, the Feast of Apip would celebrate Her nurturing and protective powers.

Today, Tawret would continue Her work as patroness of nurseries, childcare, and obstetrics. Fellow Kemetics and I have gifted pregnant friends with Tawret amulets, which were generally met with great appreciation.

Offerings: As is the case with Her colleague Bes, information about Tawret's practical worship is sparse. Milk and cool water, sweets or honey cakes would all make logical offerings. Fragrances offered may depend on which aspect of Her you wish to invoke; as patroness of maternity, floral incenses would be appropriate. To appeal to Her as a guardian of the home, offer cleansing incenses such as frankincense or cinnamon.

Feast days: Only one point in the liturgical year seems to have feasts expressly for Tawret. The feast of 'Ipet-Hemet' on the first day of *Apip* may be referring to Her, as would the eponymous feast at the end of the same month (which might be pronounced, "Uh-PEEP"). As with other deities lacking full calendars, safe bets would include honoring Tawret at New Year's, the beginnings of seasons, birth feasts for Child Gods in particular, and at year's end.

Ancient texts devoted to Tawret are practically non-existent. Much of Her liturgy had to have been oral, learned by children from their mothers and passed down. Thus, by necessity Her chant here is extremely short. But don't confuse brief with less effective; a two-line chant would be easy to memorize, and quickly called upon in a situation of need - precisely where Tawret's specialty comes in.

Chant for Tawret

Dua Tawret, notjerit a'aht
Adoration of Tawret, Great Goddess

Dua Tawret, uret hekau
Adoration of Tawret, Great of Magic

Tefnut

Tefnet

Titles:
Yarit en Ra - Uraeus of Ra
Hunet Uret - Great Young Cat

In the creation story of **Atum** (see **Ra**), He creates the first male-female pair as **Shu** and Tefnut. Her name derives from the word 'to spit', which puns one version of how Atum created Her. But don't let this seemingly crude or 'punny' origin story limit Her character. Elementally, Tefnut is described as moisture while Shu represents air; but in the Coffin Texts, She is identified as **Ma'at** while Shu is 'life'; thus, the Creator first brought into being life and truth (or cosmic order), together as the twins Shu and Tefnut. At Esna, the Creatrix **Neith** is described as the mother of Shu and Tefnut.

Pictured as a lion-headed woman, Tefnut could also act as the Eye of Ra, in the process identifying with **Wadjit** or combining with **Hathor**. When She rages in the desert, Shu must bring Her home, in one version linking with the local deity **Inhur** to do so. Once settled down, Tefnut bears the next generation of the Ennead, **Geb** and **Nut**.

Today, Tefnut has found appeal as the Mistress of atmospheric moisture, especially dew, so much more common in temperate parts of the world than in Egypt itself. Rain and rain clouds, fog, and drops of dew are seen as Her signs.

Offerings: Rose fragrance and potpourri have been cited as offerings to Tefnut. As an Eye of Ra Goddess, citrus and cinnamon flavors (in food or incense) would also be appropriate.

Feast Days: Following ten days after New Year's, Tefnut celebrated a feast in Esna. Records for Her observances become sparse after this point until May and the festival in which Shu brings Tefnut back from the desert. That said, being an Eye of Ra we can safely infer that holidays devoted to Eye Goddesses - such as Filling the Sacred Eye, and their collective Sailings in the month of *Ta'Ibet* - would have included Tefnut. The usual seasonal festivals would also apply to Her.

Chant for Tefnut

Dua Tefnut, sat Atum
Adoration of Tefnut, daughter of Atum

Dua Tefnut, sat tepyt net Neb-er-djer
Adoration of Tefnut, firstborn daughter of the Lord of All

Dua Tefnut, notjerit a'aht
Adoration of Tefnut, Great Goddess

Dua Tefnut, Irit en Ra
Adoration of Tefnut, Eye of Ra

Dua Tefnut, Yarit en Ra
Adoration of Tefnut, Uraeus of Ra

Dua Tefnut, mehenet uret
Adoration of Tefnut, Great *mehen*
[another name for the Uraeus cobra]

Dua Tefnut, hunet uret
Adoration of Tefnut, great young feline

Dua Tefnut, nebet pet
Adoration of Tefnut, Lady of the Sky

Dua Tefnut, Ma'at, Djet
Adoration of Tefnut, Ma'at, Enduring Time

Dua Tefnut, nebet ankh
Adoration of Tefnut, Lady of Life

Wadjit
Wadjyt, Ouadjet, Edjo

Titles:
Irit Ra - Eye of Ra
Imy A't-es - (She) in Her Act of Striking

The goddess Wadjit is most readily associated with the Egyptian cobra (*Naja haje*), taking the form of the Uraeus (derived from Egyptian *Yarit* or *Iaret*) cobra poised on the brow of **Ra** or the reigning king, where She is said to spit fire at Ra's enemies. But as an Eye of Ra goddess, Wadjit also possesses a leonine form. In a zoologically eclectic votive from the Late Period, a bronze statue of a seated lioness-headed goddess identified as Wadjit contains the mummy of an Egyptian mongoose (*Herpestes ichnuemon*), an animal known for its ability to kill dangerous serpents.

Wadjyt pairs with the vulture goddess **Nekhebet** to form the "Two Ladies", the tutelary goddesses of united Egypt, and as such She acts as a protectress of the state. Her center of worship lay in the Delta town of Buto, thus Wadjit could also be identified with the red crown of Lower Egypt. But on a more intimate level, Wadjit appears in combination with other solar goddesses in spells and rites of protection, either as one of a pair or as one of four "Noble Ladies" whose fiery breath dispels demons and night terrors. Spells called for clay cobras or other depictions to be placed in the four corners of a room, and actual examples have even been found among house ruins at Amarna. Given Wadjit's ancient role as a guardian against nightmares and astral intruders - even against sexual assault by demons or the vengeful dead - today She could continue to act as a formidable protectress for those who invoke Her aid. Her powers of protection might be especially valued by snake handlers as well.

Offerings: We know that in ancient times Wadjit received wine at the New Moon each month. Today, dragon's blood, sandalwood and copal incenses could be added to the traditional frankincense offering. Cinnamon and citrus would appeal to Wadjit's solar aspects. Cool water, fresh fruit, hearty breads and spicy foods would also be appropriate.

Feast Days: Thanks to a preserved stela commissioned by Thutmose III, we know of multiple holidays from Wadjit's home temple in Buto. She had four 'Feasts'; the first in September, then in November the day after Neheb-Kau; a Sailing festival three weeks later that coincided with Sailings of Bast and Hathor; a third feast in early January, which was preceded by a day of *gem bau-es*, or "The *Ba*'s are found"; then a cluster of festival observances in January and February, including a 'Feast of Entering the Sky' which may have been another type of sailing feast. The Buto calendar also informs us that the new moon and full moon were important days of offerings, and that Wadjit's temple observed the national holidays of New Year's, *Poret Sopdut* (the rising of Sirius, when that didn't coincide with civil New Year's) and the Feast of Neheb-Kau.

Wadjit's chant bears similarity to Tefnut's because of Their parallel roles.

Chant for Wadjit

Dua Wadjit, notjerit a'aht
Adoration of Wadjit, Great Goddess

Dua Wadjit, Irit en Ra
Adoration of Wadjit, Eye of Ra

Dua Wadjit, hunet uret
Adoration of Wadjit, great young feline

Dua Wadjit, Sat Ra
Adoration of Wadjit, Daughter of Ra

Dua Wadjit, imy a't-es
Adoration of Wadjit, in Her act of striking

Dua Wadjit, Yarit en Ra
Adoration of Wadjit, Uraeus of Ra

Dua Wadjit, nebet pet
Adoration of Wadjit, mistress of the sky

Dua Wadjit, nebet Pe, nebet Dep
Adoration of Wadjit, Mistress of Pe,
Mistress of Dep [towns in Buto]

Dua Wadjit, nebet Tawy
Adoration of Wadjit, Mistress of the Two Lands

Wepwawet

Up-waut, Upuaut, Ap-uat

Titles:
Up-waut - Opener of the Ways
Kherep Tawy - Controller of the Two Lands
Neb qereret - Lord of the cavern

Online comics featuring Egyptian deities often play on the fact that the canine-headed Wepwawet, who is fairly obscure outside of ardent Egyptophile circles, so closely resembles the more famous **Anubis**. Even early scholars, such as prolific early-twentieth-century author E. A. Wallis Budge, assumed that Wepwawet represented simply another aspect of Anubis, and some modern Kemetics have continued that assumption. But while the two canine deities may have acted as compliments (reflecting the Egyptians' love for duality), Wepwawet is much more than simply an aspect of Anubis, or vice versa.

His name, which means "Opener of the Ways", conveys some of His nature. Devotees describe Him as an active, protective, even 'warrior-like' God, echoing His ancient patronage of Egyptian military divisions. During the opening procession of the **Osiris** Mysteries in Abydos, Wepwawet acted as the "good son of Osiris" who led the way to Osiris's tomb and fought Osiris' enemies. Today, some of His followers report being encouraged by Him to proactively help others in need and resist bullying.

Wepwawet's canine avatar has been identified over the centuries as both a jackal and wolf. But recent mitochondrial DNA studies have determined that the 'Egyptian jackal', at one time considered a variant of the golden jackal, should actually be considered a subspecies of African wolf - hence, the Egyptian wolf, *Canis anthus lupaster*. Considering that the African wolf is itself a relative of the grey wolf, we can safely consider all of these forms of wolves to be possible animal symbols of Wepwawet.

Offerings: Modern adherents report that Wepwawet enjoys pork, unlike make other Notjeru, for whom pork is taboo. (This may come from His role as protector of Osiris, whose traditional enemy **Seth** could take the form of a boar.) Coffee and spicy cuisines have also been reported as modern offerings favored by Wepwawet. Incense offerings include frankincense, myrrh and musk. Miscellaneous offerings include camouflage printed fabrics.

Feast Days: Wepwawet was honored, and featured in procession, during the Wagy Feast and the Procession to U-Poker during the Osiris Mysteries; however, specific feasts dedicated to Him are currently a subject of research among Kemetics. Sharing holidays with Anubis would probably be too simplistic an answer. Again, based on the overall pattern of ancient holidays, the important beginnings of the year and seasons would all be appropriate times to celebrate Wepwawet.

A trove of artifacts dedicated to Wepwawet were found in His home town of Asyut in 1922, but were overlooked due to the sensational discovery of Tutankhamun's tomb. These artifacts have only recently been properly catalogued and translated, including many references to Wepwawet. Short of a full hymn from these sources, our chant for Wepwawet on the following page draws upon mostly His titles as collected from private monuments. One interpolation is 'Defender of His Father', a title often given to Horus but which also describes Wepwawet's role during the Osiris Mysteries.

Chant for Wepwawet

Dua Up-waut, notjer a'ah
Adoration of Wepwawet, Great God

Dua Up-waut, neb Ro-setau
Adoration of Wepwawet, Lord of Ro-setau

Dua Up-waut, neb qereret
Adoration of Wepwawet, Lord of the Cavern

Dua Up-waut, neb Ta-djoser
Adoration of Wepwawet, Lord of the Sacred Land

Dua Up-waut, neb Abdju
Adoration of Wepwawet, Lord of Abydos

Dua Up-waut, nedj her it-ef
Adoration of Wepwawet, Defender of His Father

Dua Up-waut, kherep Tawy
Adoration of Wepwawet, Controller of the Two Lands

The Little Ennead – Lesser-Known Deities

Aker

Aker is a cthonic deity most frequently mentioned in Underworld Texts as the guardian of caverns. He is often represented by a pair of sphinxes conjoined but facing opposite directions, with a cave at his center. In the Book of the Dead, He is described as keeping guard over hostile forces and the vanquished enemies of Ra and Osiris. An obscure deity, today He would be of most interest to those studying Egyptian magick, or *heka*.

Ammut
Ammit

The "Devourer of Souls", Ammut is known originally as a funerary deity. A composite creature formed of a hippo's rear legs, lion's front half and mane, and the head of a crocodile, She waited by the scales as the deceased were judged in the Hall of Two Truths. If an unlucky Egyptian's heart outweighed the feather of Truth, Ammut gobbled up their *ka*, or life-force. If they were judged worthy, She let them pass harmlessly into the kingdom of Osiris. While She most often comes up today in discussions of who deserves to be eaten by Her, Ammut may be making inroads into daily practice; recently one Pagan practitioner reported feeling drawn to Ammut for assistance in prayers for justice.

Anuket
Anukis

Anuket is frequently found in the company of fellow Goddess **Satit**, and Their relationship is somewhat ambiguous. In the region of Elephantine, in the extreme south of Egypt, Satit is

Anuket's mother by **Khnum**, and together They form a divine triad. But both Satit and Anuket, as well as Khnum, may be Nubian in origin. At Kawa in Nubia, Anuket was worshiped as consort to **Amun**, and Satit was Her daughter. Role-swapping with Satit aside, Anuket can be readily recognized by the bonnet full of feathers that She wears. Both Anuket and Satit were associated with the annual Nile floods, and particularly the location around the First Cataract. They both had characteristics as huntresses, but in locations where Anuket took a maternal role, She could also be pictured nursing the pharaoh, such as Rameses II at the Nubian site of Beit Al-Wali. In an interesting modern reference, Anuket (as 'Anukis') is invoked in the song, "Playing With the Big Boys" from the animated film *Prince of Egypt*.

Aton
Aten

Many modern Pagans associate Aton with the Abrahamic god YHWH/Allah, either through the belief that Atonism somehow spawned ancient Judaism, or through the two religions' common thread of monotheism. By the same token, spiritualists with a monotheistic or pantheistic view often embrace Aton as one facet of an enlightened Higher Being. Unfortunately, both views miss something of Aton's original spirit. For much of pharaonic history, Aton was viewed as simply the visibly aspect of the Creator (or even Eye of Ra Goddess, such as **Hathor**). What really made Atonism as a new religion revolutionary was its appeal - through intent if not always through practice - to the common person, doing away with complex layers of human hierarchy and intermediaries. The sun shines on everyone equally, as 'mother and father to all beings'. What spelled the Aton revolution's undoing (aside from its hostility to the established religion,) was its dependence on Akhenaton himself as sole spokesman of Aton. But just as the sun still shines, today Aton still offers His - or Its - own wisdom for anyone who seeks it.

Duamutef

One of the Four Sons of **Horus**, Duamutef's name means "Adoring His Mother" and might best be pronounced as 'doo-AH-mew-TEFF'. Usually pictured as a man with a jackal's head, He was identified with the cardinal direction of East. When acting in a funerary context, He guarded the stomach with the help of **Neith**. In modern Pagan contexts, He can act as Guardian of the East.

Hapi, Son of Horus

There are two Hapi's in Egyptian lore; first we'll discuss Hapi, one of the Four Sons of **Horus**. Taking the form of a baboon-headed man, He was identified with the cardinal direction of North, and as a protector of the dead He paired with **Nephthys** to guard the lungs. Today He can be invoked in Quarter Calls, or other magick involving the cardinal directions, as Guardian of the North.

Hapi
Hapy

Our 'other Hapi' embodied the annual Nile inundation and the agricultural bounty it brought. His image is familiar from temple scenes illustrating the various nomes of Egypt personified as fleshy-bodied men bearing offering trays heaped with bread and food. Hapi's flabby breasts - or to use a modern colloquial term, 'moobs' - and body appear androgynous, which to the ancient Egyptians conveyed fertility. This gender-ambiguous nature has resonated with a few modern Kemetics interested in "third-gender" or gender-neutral archetypes.

Hat-Mehyt

Her name means "At the fore of the fishes," and She was represented as either a Nile carp (*Labeo niloticus*) or a woman with a carp above Her head. (Scholars at one time mis-identified it as a dolphin.) At Her center of worship in the Delta town of Mendes, Her consort was the ram-headed god Banebdjedet. In modern Kemeticism, Hat-Mehyt has received some attention from Reconstructionists interested in obscure deities.

Heka

Formed by the Creator at the First Time, Heka embodies the force that today we would call 'magick'. (Among Pagans, the word is spelled with a -k to distinguish serious Craft work from stage magic.) Heka is the creative power used to fashion the world, which was then given to humankind so that they could protect themselves. As a deity, Heka is commonly pictured as a man wearing divine attributes (kilt, bull's tail, divine beard) and holding two wavy snakes. Most often Heka is thought of as the child and attribute of **Ra**, but in the temple at Esna, He was regarded as the son of **Neith** and part of Her Ennead. While Heka as a deity was not specifically invoked in ancient spells, modern practitioners of magick might choose to invoke His aid. He is also invoked as one of the Four Virtues of Ra, alongside **Hu**, **Sia** and **Ma'at**.

Heqat
Hekat, Heqet

A friendly goddess known for Her gifts of fertility and assisting women in labor, Heqet is usually pictured as a frog or frog-headed woman. She often occurs as a counterpart to **Khnum**. In a Middle Kingdom legend, Heqet appeared in disguise as part of a 'dancing troupe' with Khnum, **Isis**, **Nephthys** and Meskhenet - another birth-Goddess who embodied the bricks women sat on to give birth - in order to assist the birth of three sons destined to become famous pharaohs. (The story is a complete historical fiction, but is fascinating nonetheless.) By virtue of Her skills as a midwife, Heqat was invoked to help the dead attain rebirth. In Khemnu, She was associated with **Nehmetaway** as a mother Goddess, and with the Ogdoad, or Eight Primeval Gods. (The place name Khemnu meant "Eight-Town".) The "Mistress of Joy", Heqat also shared a temple, now in ruins, with Elder **Horus** in the town of Qus. But She has found new followers today, and is reported to enjoy rain-scented candles and fresh, green fruits.

Hu

Hu's name is translated as authority or as "Authoritative Speech". He is associated with the left ear or the left side of the body. Together with **Sia**, he emerged from the blood of **Ra**-Atum when He circumcised Himself. Hu, his twin Sia and the god **Heka**, or magick, assisted Ra in creating the ordered universe. Hu and Sia stand on the solar barge to assist Ra in his daily voyage through the sky and nightly passage through the underworld. Today, He is invoked as one of the Four Virtues of Ra.

Inhur
Onuris, Anhur, Inhert

Hailing from the ancient town of Thinis (or This), Inhur was a hunter and warrior god whose name means 'Brings back the distant one'. That 'distant one' was a lioness goddess roaming the desert; in local tradition it was Mehit, who became His consort. In later tradition She was identified as **Hathor-Tefnut**, and Inhur with **Shu**. Carrying a harpoon and length of rope and wearing a divine beard and crown of four plumes, Inhur was also invoked against evil forces and said to battle a malevolent crocodile named Maga.

Ihy

A child god and son of **Hathor**, Ihy is pictured as a naked boy wearing a sidelock and holding a sistrum. His name is rendered as 'Musician', and He shares His mother's affinity for music. Ihy is also identified with **Horus** in His aspect of the Child, or as Harsomtus, *Hor-Sema-Tawy* ('Horus Uniter of the Two Lands).

Imsety

His name has been translated as 'He of the Dill'. Pictured as a man, Imsety is one of the Four Sons of **Horus** associated with the cardinal direction of South. As a funerary deity, He typically paired with **Isis** to protect the mummified liver of the deceased. In modern Pagan contexts, He can be invoked during Quarter Calls as Guardian of the South.

Maahes
Mahes, Mihos, Myusis

The son of **Bastet** and **Atum-Ra**, Maahes took the form of a lion or lion-headed man. At Per-Bastet, He formed a divine triad with Bastet and Ra; elsewhere, He was described as son of **Sakhmet** and **Ptah,** and associated with **Nefertum**. A warrior deity who defended Ra and the reigning king against enemies, Maahes shared similarities with the Nubian god **Apademak**. By Hellenistic times He took on additional associations with storms.

Of all the relatively obscure deities in Egyptian religion, Maahes seems to have found a fairly high level of interest among modern Pagans. Statues of Him brandishing swords can be found online. He is invoked as a giver of strength and courage who removes obstacles. Some Pagans have even suggested He has a bisexual nature; but lacking further research (or corroborated reports), this aspect must be taken as personal gnosis.

Mafdet
Maftet

A feline Goddess, Mafdet is pictured in royal imagery going as far back as the First dynasty. Her specialty was protecting the king and Her worshipers from snakes and scorpions, clawing out the eyes of serpents in Her form of either an Egyptian mongoose (*Herpestes ichneumon*) or African wildcat (*Felis lybica*). In yet another random reference from modern pop culture, Mafdet appears as a male 'lynx god' in the classic 1980's cartoon, *Thundercats*.

Meretseger

Her name meaning "She Loves Silence", Meretseger was worshiped by the villagers of Deir el-Medina. A cobra goddess who presided over the Valley of the Kings, she was also referred to as the "Peak of the West". Some of the artisans who worked in Her domain commissioned heartfelt works of piety and repentance dedicated to Her; one votive stela by a certain Neferabu - who describes an affliction reminiscent of passing a kidney stone - warns, "The Peak strikes with the stroke of a savage lion, She is after him who offends Her!"

Montu

Monthu, Mont, Month

Having the head of a falcon and wearing twin plumes - or, when assimilated with **Ra**, a sun disc and two plumes - Montu was primarily associated with warfare and protection of the king in battle. His worship centered in the small towns of Tod, Medamud and Armant which surround Thebes. The modern Arabic name of 'Armant' echoes the name of Montu. He took a three- or fourfold form, His image being painted in fours on the prow of Egyptian warships.

References in the Pyramid Texts to stars suggest that Montu may have held a place in the Egyptian constellations. His consorts were either Tjenenyt or **Ra'et-Tawy**, and the Buchis bulls were considered His earthly manifestation. Veneration of the Buchis bulls continued into Roman times. Although not frequently invoked today, Montu's patronage would cover servicemen, the armed forces and martial arts.

Nefertum
Nefertem

The son of **Ptah** and **Sakhmet**, or occasionally **Bastet**, Nefertum was associated with the Egyptian blue lily (*Nymphaea caerulea*) and perfumes. He could act as a Child God, parallel to **Horus** or **Khonsu**; appear as a grown man with a lotus emblem on His head, or be interpreted as a primeval lotus out of which **Ra** emerged. His roles are poorly understood today, but His greatest interest may lie in the reputed psychotropic effects of his sacred plant, Egyptian blue lily.

Nehmetawai
Nehmetaway

Nehmetawai was a lioness-headed goddess worshiped in certain regions as the consort of **Djehuty** (Thoth). As 'She Who Restores What Is Lost', Nehmetawai punished thieves and wrongdoers. Like other leonine goddesses, She could act as the Eye of Ra or work in concert with fellow Eye goddesses such as **Sakhmet, Bastet** and **Pakhet** to form a four-fold magickal protection. In the Egyptian region of Khemnu, She could be identified with **Heqat**.

Nekhebet
Nekhbet

'She of Nekheb', an ancient capital of Upper Egypt, most often Nekhebet is encountered as the vulture on queens' crowns or alongside Her fellow tutelary Goddess, **Wadjit**. As a pair, They were addressed as the 'Two Ladies'. Nekhebet could be pictured as a fully human woman wearing the white crown of

Upper Egypt, as well as a vulture, a cobra, or a long-horned cow; in this last role, She nursed the infant **Horus** and took on motherly roles. The Greeks and Romans identified Her with their goddess Eileithya, in which guise the worship of Nekhebet continued into the early centuries C.E.

Nun
Nu, Noun

Nun is the primordial ocean from which the creator god emerged. An infinite, dark expanse, Nun still surrounds the created world and can perhaps be understood today as outer space (or even dark matter). When **Ra** descends to the Underworld, or *Duat*, He returns to Nun in order regenerate. Personified, Nun was the eldest divinity, the father of Ra who gave Him counsel in the "Book of the Celestial Cow". As a concept, Nun embodies beginnings, regeneration, and unknown potential.

Pakhet

A lioness goddess whose name has been rendered as "She who scratches" or even "Tearer-Apart", Pakhet had a rock-cut temple dedicated to her in the Middle Egyptian town of Beni Hasan (modern Arabic name). Greeks called Her temple *Speos Artemidos*, the 'Cave of Artemis', identifying Pakhet with Artemis. An inscription dedicated by Hatshepsut at Speos Artemidos invokes "Pakhet, who roams the wadis, who resides in the Eastern Desert", and Hatshepsut may have renovated Pakhet's temple as part of a broader emphasis on solar goddesses in general. In the "Book of Overthrowing 'Apep'", Pakhet is invoked alongside Sakhmet as burning the evil serpent in Her flame. Claw amulets, often found in Middle Kingdom jewelry troves, may have invoked Pakhet's protective power.

Qebehsenuef
Kebehsenuf, Qebsenuf

His name means, "He cools His brothers", referring specifically to cooling waters. Qebehsenuef - perhaps best pronounced as KEB-eh-SEN-yoo-EFF - was one of the Four Sons of Horus, associated with the cardinal direction of West. He was pictured as a human with a falcon's head, or sometimes fully human. In funerary contexts, He was guarded by **Serket** and housed the intestines of the mummified dead. Today, He can be invoked in modern Pagan Quarter Calls as Guardian of the West; in this case, His association with water proves rather apt.

Ra'et-Tawy

A female doublet of **Ra**, Ra'et-Tawy - 'Female Ra of the Two Lands' - borrowed much of **Hathor**'s iconography and may have initially been considered an aspect of Her. By the New Kingdom, Ra'et-Tawy had come to be worshiped as an independent goddess. In the region of Armant, Ra'et-Tawy was the consort of the war god **Montu**, who could also be linked to Ra. An extremely fragmentary hymn in Demotic from the Roman period invokes Ra'et-Tawy as "Our mistress, the one who makes everything", suggesting that Her importance had grown quite considerably. Today, those looking for a more feminine aspect of the familiar sun god could certainly find one in Ra'et-Tawy.

Rennutet
Renenutet, Ernutet, Thermouthis

Rennutet is a cobra goddess of the harvest. In agrarian Egypt, cobras served a purpose by hunting the rats and vermin that would threaten crops. In this serpentine guise, Rennutet brings bountiful harvests and nourishes humankind. A mother goddess, she nourishes the grain, personified as the god Nepri (or Neper). She is also pictured as a cobra-headed woman suckling a child. By Hellenistic times, She absorbed into **Isis** to form the local variant Isis-Thermouthis. Today, American Thanksgiving would fall under Her purview - although the image of a cobra amongst the cornucopia (itself an ancient pagan symbol) might surprise a few dinner guests..!

Satit
Satet, Satis

Companion to **Anuket**, Satit acted as Her mother in some locations (such as Elephantine) and daughter in others (such as Kawa, Nubia). Satit wore the white crown of Upper Egypt framed by gazelle's horns. Huntress and guardian of the First Cataract region, She carried a bow and arrows and heralded the coming of the Inundation. She was linked to Sirius, the star whose appearance coincided with the annual floods. Satit's consorts included **Khnum** in southern Egypt and **Amun** in Nubia. As suggested by Her crown, gazelles were sacred to Her.

Sia

His name is typically rendered as Perception or Insight. Along with **Hu**, Sia sprang from the Creator and guides Him from the prow of the sun barge. Sia is associated with the right ear or the right side of the body and bestows wisdom. In a religious text known as Coffin Text 335 and in later form as Book of the Dead Spell 17, Sia gives **Ra** His identity of the Great Tomcat by saying "how like Him, by what He has done" - punning the Egyptian words *mi*, 'like' and *miu*, 'cat'. Today, Sia is invoked as one of the Four Virtues of Ra.

Ta'it
Tait, Tayet

Ta'it is a goddess of weaving. She is invoked in the Pyramid Texts and in morning ritual addresses. Sometimes paired with another, more obscure weaver Goddess named Hadj-hotep, She is credited with weaving mummy wrappings and sacred garments.

Tatenen
Tatjenen, Ta-tenen

Tatenen embodies the Primeval Mound, which was the first ground to emerge from the waters of **Nun**, as well as the depths of the earth. He most frequently combined with **Ptah** to form the composite Ptah-Tatenen. In art, He could be pictured as fully human or as a mound of earth with a head rising from it. In modern Paganism, the book *Circle of Isis* identifies a 'Tameran earth goddess' called 'Tanent', which could be a misreading of Tatenen.

Tutu
Tithoes

Great God
Great of Valor
Chief of the Emissaries (or **Master of Demons**)
Son of Neith

Tutu seems to have appeared relative late in Egyptian history. Pictured as a sphinx wearing royal crowns, Tutu embodied protection and ferocity. At Esna, He was honored as "Chief of the Emissaries" and the "Son of **Neith**". These 'Emissaries' were also known as the 'Messengers' or 'Arrows' of **Sakhmet**, demonic forces who could inflict plague and misfortune. Tutu was invoked as their master who held power over them and could prevent them from causing harm. His popularity increased during the Roman era, to the point where He took on a fully human form and the local consorts **Isis** of Shenhur and the goddess Tapshay in Dakhla Oasis. His worship is documented into the fourth century C.E. Today, the many sphinx figurines so commonly found in curio and metaphysical stores could be interpreted as symbols of Tutu.

Wennut
Wenut, Unut

Fittingly, we reach one of the most obscure deities at the end. A goddess local to Khemnu, hometown of **Djehuty**, Wennut's name is spelled with a rabbit hieroglyph and She came to be pictured as a rabbit-headed woman - hence Her epithet among some modern Kemetics, 'the Bunny Goddess'. But there's *another* Wennut, the 'Goddess of the Hours', more commonly invoked during solar rituals observing the passage of the hours. Until the ancient solar litanies of the hours can be better articulated for modern Pagan practice, this Wennut is more likely to be invoked in contests of trivia knowledge among Kemetics.

The Nubian Ennead

Like much of Nubia's history and surviving archaeological sites, her native deities are obscure and under-documented. Various factors contribute to this imbalance. Most importantly, we still have not completely deciphered the Nubian language; even now scholars work to decode monuments written in Meroitic script, the alphabet developed during the Meroitic period of Nubian history. Also, Egypt's enduring fame has far eclipsed Nubia's since the time of the Greeks and Romans. And finally, surviving temples are often in poor states of preservation because of the soft native sandstone in which they were built; flooding from the Aswan High Dam has completely submerged many other sites, and still more are under threat from new dam projects being built in North Sudan.

But this section is meant to redress the balance in small measure, and give readers interested in the native Gods and Goddesses of Nubia a starting point for their own exploration. Entries are given for deities that have some amount of relatable information. But there are others for whom we know little more than names and passing references. An inscription from the official Haramadeye of Karanog names several deities of whom we know little else: Ariten, Amanete, Mash and Makedeke. May Their stories come to light in the near future.

Amesemi

The native consort of **Apademak**, Amesemi was only recently rediscovered, pictured on a plaque discovered in 2000 at the Nubian site of Naqa. Further work indicates that Amesemi could appear with either short curly hair or a close-fitting cap bearing a crescent with twin falcons.

Apademak

Pictured as a lion-headed man in royal regalia, or more rarely as a serpent with a man's torso and arms with a lion's head, Apademak was among the most important of the native Nubian Gods. A creator on par with **Amun**, Apademak hailed from the southern Nubian region of Butana, in which the late-era capital city of Meroe was located. Apademak bestowed fertility, defended the land and king (or queen) against their enemies and endowed the right of legitimacy to new rulers. He carried a bow and arrows, conveying His warrior nature, but also had associations with water and the nourishing Nile floods. Apademak could be paired with **Amesemi** or with **Isis**; in those instances, Isis took on some of His warlike aspects. The Lion Temple in Naqa, a major site of the Meroitic Period, is dedicated to Him. We know more about Apademak than many other Nubian deities because texts to Him were written in Egyptian, which had been adopted as court language by the Napatan kings. His titles included, "Splendid God at the Head of Nubia," "Lion of the South," and "Strong of Arm". Access was unavailable at the time of press, but interested readers can look for *Apedemak: lion god of Meroe* by L. V. Zakbar for more information about this fascinating God.

Aqedise

An obscure lunar deity, Aqedise may be a Nubian parallel to **Khonsu**.

Arensnuphis

Arensnuphis is the Greek form of the Egyptian name *Iry Hemes Nofer*, or 'Good Companion'. Scholars debate whether He originated in Egypt or Nubia. Taking either human or lion form,

Arensnuphis was also worshiped alongside **Isis** at Philae, the famous island in southern Egypt that received Nubian pilgrimages and support well into the Christian era. Further south into Nubia, Arensnuphis frequently paired with the more obscure lion god **Sebiumeker**. They were pictured as guardians flanking temple entrances.

Mandulis

A sun god who paralleled both **Ra** and **Horus**, Mandulis (or Merwel) was pictured as a human-headed falcon, sometimes alongside His twin brother Breith. He had a temple at Kalabsha, south of Aswan, Egypt, which may have first been built during the New Kingdom but is best known from its Roman-era renovation. Pilgrims from as far north as Alexandria came to worship Mandulis at Kalabsha, and they equated Him with the Greek deity Aion or addressed Him as the 'son of Zeus'. Religious associations (Greek *sunodoi*) dedicated to Mandulis remained active into the fifth century C.E. Mandulis is also pictured, along with **Arensnuphis**, in the rescued temple of Dendur that is now located in the Metropolitan Museum in New York.

Sebiumeker

Frequent companion to His 'Good Friend' **Arensnuphis**, Sebiumeker shared His leonine and hunter-warrior aspects. The name 'Sebiumeker' is actually Egyptian; scholars believe that the native Nubian form of His name was Sabomakal. He was associated with the Egyptian creator **Atum**, and as such Sebiumeker bestowed life. When He took human form, He wore a traditional royal kilt, the Egyptian dual crown and divine beard.

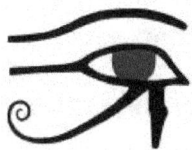

A Calendar of Feast Days

The calendar in this chapter lists many of the feast days honoring Notjeru we have discussed. Lengthy though it is, however, our list does not cover anywhere near the entirety of ancient Egyptian festivals. Each ancient temple had its own full year of observances, many of them unique to that location. In trying to formulate a modern liturgical calendar, the best approach to maintain coherence (and sanity) I've found is to concentrate on major festivals and recurring themes. If you have an interest in further researching holidays for a particular deity, be sure to check the Online Resources and Bibliography. But first, let's review some basic 'ground rules' on ancient Egyptian holiday schedules.

Understanding the Egyptian Liturgical Year

Egyptian months here are given by name, much as we would list our own 'January', 'February', etc. But most scholarly sources do not follow this format. Rather, they give Egyptian months by the number of the month in its season, then date - so, for example, 'I Akhet 1' for the first day of the year, then 'I Akhet 2', and so on. The ancients themselves used this system predominantly until the Late Period, but month names are known from as far back as the Middle Kingdom. Named months, in my experience, are easier to learn and less abstract than using numbers; but should you consult an academic article or book (something I always encourage), you'll need to know the Egyptian year 'by the numbers'. If you've already read *Circle of the Sun,* just consider this part a recap:

First Season - Akhet, or Flood
I Akhet - Djehutet
II Akhet - Pa'en-Opet
III Akhet - Hat-Hor
IV Akhet - Ka-Hor-Ka

Second Season - Poret, or Emergence
(also called 'winter')
I Poret - Ta'ibet
II Poret - Makhir
III Poret - Pa'en-Amunhotepu
IV Poret - Pa'en-Rennutet

Third Season - Shomu, or Summer
I Shomu - Pa-Khonsu
II Shomu - Pa'en-Inet
III Shomu - Apip
IV Shomu - Mosu-Ra

Hence, the calendar of feast days starts with Djehutet 1, which is Egyptian New Year's Day - commonly called *Wep Ronpet* among Kemetic Pagans, though here given the variant spelling *Upet Ronpet*. So what date is Egyptian New Year's on our modern calendar?

That depends on which Kemetic tradition you choose to follow. Just as Eastern Orthodox Christians observe their Christmas and Easter at different dates from Roman Catholic and Protestant Christians, Kemetics have alternate ways of reckoning the start of their liturgical year. All of these methods have in common the rising of Sirius - also known today as the "Dog Star" (think of the Sirius XM logo) - in the predawn sky during late summer. The Kemetic Orthodox bases its New Year on the forecasted rising of Sirius over its 'Mother Shrine' (and 'Royal Residence') in Joliet, Illinois, USA. This date can vary by a few days following a leap year, and online questions about timing for Kemetic Orthodox events come up quite frequently. Kemetic Reconstructionists use dates for the local rising of Sirius, depending on where an individual practitioner lives. This also varies, not only because of leap year shifts, but also because Sirius' appearance comes at different times depending on one's longitude. Generally speaking, the further west of Egypt someone lives, the later Sirius rises in the summer for their area. (Reconstructionists living on the same line of longitude as Chicago, IL, will have dates that coincide with the Orthodox's calendar.) Kemetics living outside of North America often have a more difficult time calculating their start date, though web resources can help make the process somewhat easier.

If you've read *Following the Sun* and *Circle of the Sun*, though, you'll already be familiar with the Kemetic Reform reckoning of New Year's. Rather than struggle with modern local rise dates for Sirius, the Kemetic Reform calendar uses the historical rising of Sirius, which took place on July 18th in New Kingdom Egypt. By keeping a fixed date relative to the modern calendar, this method also accounts for leap years, without causing any shift from one year to the next. This central start date also allows more Kemetics in distant parts of the globe to participate together for major holidays, even if 'together' only means through online connections. It also echoes the date used by the Church of the Eternal Source, which hosted Egyptian New Year's parties in Los Angeles, California every July 18th beginning in the 1960's. The CES was the first Egyptian Pagan group to become legally recognized, so their observance offers a valid precedent.

(Pagans following a more mainstream form of Egyptian practice such as Tameran Wicca or Isian tradition will also find the revised edition of *Following the Sun* helpful in adapting a Wheel of the Year, which differs substantially from the Kemetic year.)

As you read the table of feast dates, the ancient festival with its Egyptian date is given in the left-hand column. The corresponding Kemetic Reform date occurs in the middle column. To the far right you will see the approximate Kemetic Orthodox equivalent; again, their dates change from year to year, so this column is given strictly as a point of reference and is by no means authoritative (nor an endorsement). In parentheses below that, you will find an equivalent date for Reconstructionists, based on a heliacal rising of Sirius on the West Coast of the United States, where a majority of active Reconstructionist groups are based. While these equivalencies cannot account for every variation of Kemetic year - the group Amentet Neferet uses an entirely different start date, for example - they cover some of the most common systems used and can facilitate their comparison.

What the list cannot convey so easily, however, is the relative importance of festivals. Certain Egyptian feasts were celebrated nationally as major holidays, while others remained quite localized. Our calendar here combines references from temples across Egypt, spanning chronologically from the Middle Kingdom through the Greco-Roman period, as well as the Cairo Calendar of 'Lucky and Unlucky Days'. Because of these eclectic sources, certain festival events (such as the Raising of the *Djed-*

pillar or Chewing Onions for Bastet) will appear to be duplicated; in actuality, the multiple dates often indicate regional variations of a theme. This occurs especially frequently with national deities who possessed a number of local avatars, such as Horus, who celebrated His birthday several times throughout the year.

We can ascertain a few general guidelines about the Egyptian liturgical cycle. New Year's Day, *Upet Ronpet*, was one of the most important holidays of the year and involved a major procession and "Union with the sun" at every temple. Likewise, the last day of the year - the Day of *Mosyt*, which probably referred to the evening meal - also occasioned numerous processions, celebrations and the lighting of torches. The opening of a new season also called for major observances. The first day of Poret, beginning the month of Ta'ibet, was actually treated as a 'second New Year's Day'. Temples throughout Egypt observed the Feast of Neheb-kau on that date, although Horus' domain at Edfu added its own flavor with the Coronation of the Sacred Falcon. Later in the year, the start of Shomu marked the beginning of harvest season, occasioning a plethora of feasts for mother- and child-deities, and Amun's procreative aspect as Amun-Min. Other festivals with national relevance include the Osiris-Sokar, or Khoiakh Mysteries, which took place over several days and for which we have extensive documentation; the Opet Festival, also a multi-day holiday in which Amun took center stage; and to a slightly lesser extent, the Feast of the Beautiful Reunion between Hathor of Denderah and Horus of Edfu. Ancient dates for both the Beautiful Reunion and the Beautiful Feast of the Valley were determined by the new moon, which meant their exact date varied from year to year. Certain dates given in our present calendar are marked as 'approximate' for this reason.

Another bit of advice when reading the list of dates: don't try to observe *every* feast day! Grab a highlighter and pick out ones relevant to your patron Gods or Goddesses, or consider the major holidays just described. If you try to celebrate all or even a majority of these dates, you won't have time to do much of anything else the rest of the year.

Observances Then and Now

The transition from ancient to modern times has given rise to new interpretations of holidays, and morphed a handful of lesser-known feast days into popular Kemetic themes - if not outright memes. A prime example would be the Feast of Establishing the Celestial Cow, which is known primarily from the Cairo Calendar and seems to have been a relatively minor observance in ancient Egypt. It reflects the resolution of the Myth of Destruction of Mankind, in which Nut took the form of a 'Heavenly Cow' and raised Ra into the heavens. On the Kemetic Orthodox calendar, this observance often coincides with modern Christmas; several online forum jokes and blatant parodies of Yuletide classics later, and the Feast of Establishing the Celestial Cow has become "Moomas". Another holiday documented from the Ptolemaic era that has been adopted into the Orthodox calendar, though in a form that puzzles other Kemetics, is their "Feast of Cucumbers for Sekhmet". In the calendar for Hathor recorded at the temple of Edfu, this entry is given:

> **Day 14.** Feast of registration for a day. Removing the tie and unrolling her papyri, by this goddess, while the women of this town/domain take *Menat*-collars in their hands to gladden everyone, singing: "Osiris is well, and Tebeh (Seth) is no more!"
> Cucumbers go forth from him (Osiris?). It is the Eye of Horus that munches them; it is Horus thirsty(?) in the desert(?) that munches them; (so) does the priest of Sekhmet (also) munch cucumbers before her.
> - *in El-Sabban, "The Temple Calendars of Ancient Egypt"*

Here we run into the common problem of deciphering an ambiguous text. Because the entry is part of a larger calendar for Hathor, and says 'this goddess', presumably it refers to Hathor. Shaking *menat* necklaces as a form of instrument certainly links to Hathor, and by Ptolemaic times She could be identified as either the Eye of Ra or the Eye of Horus. But the Kemetic Orthodox treats Hathor and Sakhmet as the same Goddess, whom they call 'Het-hert-Sekhmet', so reference to one Goddess is automatically conflated with the other. The original Ptolemaic entry calls for a 'priest of Sekhmet' to eat cucumbers in front of 'her' - not specifying whether that 'her' is Hathor or Sakhmet. It could have been either Goddess, because at Esna's feast on the first of Pa'Inet, temple records called for a priest of Sakhmet to officiate before Khnum and Neith in an execration ritual. Evidently the priest did not have to perform exclusively for his ordained deity; perhaps he had special training that came into use for other occasions. But these considerations notwithstanding, a day of offering and eating cucumbers for Horus and an Eye Goddess has morphed into the Orthodox's holiday of "Cucumbers for Sekhmet".

Of course, all Kemetic traditions face the same problems with interpretation as other types of Pagan Reconstructionist faiths - and regardless of the jargon we use amongst ourselves, all Kemetic groups fall on a continuum of Reconstructionism. What allows us the illusion of being different from, for example, Celtic or Hellenic Reconstructionism is that so many ancient Egyptian hymns and ritual texts have survived. We've found enough written records from the Egyptians to put together a rough picture, but that picture still leaves many pieces missing.

Destruction of physical relics aside, another reason for this is human limitation; no one ever thinks to write an instruction manual about the holidays they grow up knowing how to take part in. To illustrate by analogy, imagine if someone from two thousand years into the future tried to throw a traditional

Western Christmas party. All they had to go on were translations of parts of the New Testament in their own language, and a few artistic renderings of Christmas parties. If those pictures included Santa Claus, would our future Reconstructionist confuse Santa with Jesus? Would they offer cookies and milk or eggnog to Jesus on Christmas Eve? And what about all those annoying Christmas songs - a future celebrant would miss that defining element (be that good or ill) of the Christmas season. Their own rendition would probably still be quite sincere, but it would not resemble what we know today.

Thus, our feast days for the Notjeru will not identically resemble their pharaonic antecedents because they cannot. In moving forward with Egyptian - now Kemetic - practice and renewing observances for the Gods, we can take one of three possible strategies. The first is to remain defined by what we lack, through strictly adhering to only those elements (text translations, food and beverage offerings, etc.) that match surviving records. Another is to graft what we know of pharaonic practice onto existing systems; Tameran Wicca often gets criticized for this, but the Kemetic Orthodox borrows heavily from Haitian Voudon, Coptic Orthodox Christian elements and, as described above, modern meme culture.

The remaining strategy, which I advocate, is to carefully balance research with our modern lives and needs. This approach takes many forms, such as the deity chants, which were inspired by similar Asian practices without copying them wholesale. Taken together, I envision this strategy building a Kemetic practice that faithfully reflects its ancient predecessor while being very much a product of our time. With that in mind, let's look at our calendar.

Ancient Holiday	Kemetic Reform Date	Kemetic Orthodox (Reconstructionist)
Djehutet 1 - Upet Ronpet (Egyptian New Year)	July 18	August 3 (August 7)
Djehutet 2 - Going forth of Ihy	July 19	August 4 (August 8)
Poret Sopdut	July 25	no equivalent
Djehutet 9 - Going Forth of Hathor	July 26	August 11 (August 15)
Djehutet 10 - Feast of Tefnut at Esna	July 27	August 12 (August 16)
Djehutet 17-18 - Wagy Feast	August 3-4	August 19-20 (August 23-24)
Djehutet 19 - Feast of Djehutet	August 5	August 21 (August 25)
Djehutet 20 - Purification of Ra	August 6	August 22 (August 26)

Ancient Holiday	Kemetic Reform Date	Kemetic Orthodox (Reconstructionist)
Djehutet 21 - Feast of Tekhy (Drunkenness)	August 7	August 23 (August 29)
Djehutet 22 - Going Forth of Osiris; Feast of Anubis in Denderah	August 8	August 24 (August 30)
Djehutet 30 - Feast of Osiris and His Ennead in Abydos	August 16	September 1 (September 5)
Pa'en-Opet 2 - Elder Horus Goes Forth to Visit Neith	August 18	September 3 (September 7)
Pa-en-Opet 3 - Feast of Sobek, Lord of Ombos	August 19	September 4 (September 8)
Pa'en-Opet 6 - Feast of Isis the Great	August 22	September 7 (September 11)
Pa'en-Opet 9 - Sailing of Horus of Behdet	August 25	September 10 (September 14)

Ancient Holiday	Kemetic Reform Date	Kemetic Orthodox (Reconstructionist)
Pa'en-Opet 10 - Procession of Bastet, Mistress of Ankh-Tawy	August 26	September 11 (September 15)
Pa'en-Opet 16 - Feasts of Unnofer, Neith	September 1	September 17 (September 21)
Pa'en-Opet 17, 27 - Robing of Anubis; Feast of Montu, **Day 27**	September 2, 12 September 12	September 18, 28 (Sept. 22, Oct. 2)
Pa'en-Opet 18 - Feast of Khnum and Anuket	September 3	September 19 (September 23)
Pa'en-Opet 18-25 - Opet Feast	September 3-10	September 19-26 (September 23-30)
Pa'en-Opet 24 - Moving Sand for Anubis	September 9	September 25 (September 29)
Pa'en-Opet 28 - Feast of Satit and Anuket at Elephantine	September 13	September 29 (October 3)

Ancient Holiday	Kemetic Reform Date	Kemetic Orthodox (Reconstructionist)
Hat-Hor 1 - Feast of Sakhmet in Esna	September 16	October 1 (October 5)
Hat-Hor 3 - First Feast of Wadjit	September 18	October 3 (October 7)
Hat-Hor 8 - Isis Goes Forth in Joy	September 23	October 9 (October 13)
Hat-Hor 9 - Feast of Amun	September 24	October 10 (October 14)
Hat-Hor 10 - Feast of Neith and Tutu at Esna	September 25	October 11 (October 15)
Hat-Hor 17 - Isis and Nephthys mourn Osiris; Feast of Amun after Opet	October 2	October 18 (October 22)
Hat-Hor 21 - Feast of Shu, Son of Ra	October 6	October 22 (October 26)
Hat-Hor 22 - Ma'at is Raised Up to Ra	October 7	October 23 (October 27)

Ancient Holiday	Kemetic Reform Date	Kemetic Orthodox (Reconstructionist)
Hat-Hor 24 - Isis Goes Forth, Nephthys is in Joy	October 9	October 25 (October 29)
Hat-Hor 28 - Feast of Hathor Residing-in-Ombos	October 13	October 29 (November 2)
Hat-Hor 29-Ka-Hor-Ka 1 - Feast of Horus of Behdet (Edfu)	October 14-16	October 30 - November 1 (November 3 -5)
Hat-Hor 30 - Sailing of Hathor, Revealing Bosoms of Women	October 15	October 31 (November 4)
Ka-Hor-Ka 1 - Ra is Joyful; Feast of Hathor, Offerings to Amun-Ra	October 16	November 1 (November 5)
Ka-Hor-Ka 4 - Perform Rites to Sobek	October 19	November 4 (November 8)
Ka-Hor-Ka 5 - Appearance of Neith	October 20	November 5 (November 9)

Ancient Holiday	Kemetic Reform Date	Kemetic Orthodox (Reconstructionist)
Ka-Hor-Ka 11 - Feast of Osiris in Abydos	October 26	November 11 (November 15)
Ka-Hor-Ka 15 - Feast of Sakhmet and Bastet	October 30	November 15 (November 19)
Ka-Hor-Ka 18-30 - Osiris Mysteries:	**November 2-14:**	**November 18-30 (Nov. 22 - Dec. 4):**
Ka-Hor-Ka 20 - Purifying the Ennead	November 4	Nov. 20 (Nov. 24)
Ka-Hor-Ka 22- Hacking the Earth	November 6	Nov. 22 (Nov. 26)
Ka-Hor-Ka 25 - Day of *Notjeryt*	November 9	Nov. 25 (Nov. 29)
Ka-Hor-Ka 26-27 - Unions of Neith and Hathor with Sun Disc; Feast of Sokar, **Day 26**	November 10-11 November 11	Nov. 26-27 (Nov. 30 - Dec.1) Nov. 26 (Nov. 30)
Ka-Hor-Ka 28 - Drawing Forth the *Benben*	November 12	Nov. 28 (Dec. 2)
Ka-Hor-Ha 30 - Raising the *Djed*	November 14	Nov. 30 (Dec. 4)

Ancient Holiday	Kemetic Reform Date	Kemetic Orthodox (Reconstructionist)
Ta'ibet 1 - Coronation of the Sacred Falcon, Hab Sed, Feast of Neheb-Kau	November 15	December 1 (December 5)
Ta'ibet 2 - Second Feast of Wadjit	November 16	December 2 (December 6)
Ta'ibet 3 - Drunkenness in Edfu	November 17	December 3 (December 7)
Ta'ibet 16 - Shu Goes Forth	November 30	December 16 (December 20)
Ta'ibet 18-21 - Feasts of Neith on Her Lake, Heka; Holiday in Ro-setau, **Day 18**	December 2-5 December 2	December 18-21 (December 22-25) Dec. 18 (Dec. 20)
Ta'ibet 20 - Sailing of Bast, Wadjit; Hathor of Denderah, **Days 19-21**	December 4 December 3-5	Dec. 20 (Dec. 24) December 19-21 (December 23-25)
Ta'ibet 25 - Establishing the Celestial Cow	December 9	December 25 (December 29)

	Kemetic Reform Date	Kemetic Orthodox (Reconstructionist)
...uty ... Solemn Oath in Khemnu	December 12	December 28 (January 1)
Ta'ibet 30 - Sailing of Mut	December 14	December 30 (January 3)
Makhir 1 - Ptah Lifts the Sky; Sailing of Anubis in Djeme	December 15	December 31 (January 4)
Makhir 6 - Raising the *Djed* for Osiris in Abydos; Feasts of Shu, Sakhmet	December 20	January 5 (January 9)
Makhir 8 - Opening the Doors of the House of Neith in Sais	December 22	January 7 (January 11)
Makhir 9 - Amun Lifts the Sky; Feast of the Great Burning (*Rekh-Ur*)	December 23	January 8 (January 12)
Makhir 10 - Ra raises Ma'at	December 24	January 9 (January 13)

Ancient Holiday	Kemetic Reform Date	Kemetic Orthodox (Reconstructionist)
Makhir 11 - Sobek Goes Forth, Feast of Neith	December 25	January 10 (January 14)
Makhir 16 - Awakening of Isis	December 30	January 15 (January 19)
Makhir 17 - Feasts of Min, Lord of Sais, Neith, Anubis	December 31	January 16 (January 20)
Makhir 21-25 - Feast of Victory of Horus; Third Feast of Wadjit, **Day 25**	January 4-8 January 8	January 20-24 (January 24-28) Jan. 24 (Jan. 28)
Makhir 26 - Min Goes Forth to Coptos	January 9	January 25 (January 29)
Makhir 27-28 - Feasts of Sokar in Ro-setau, Unnofer	January 10-11	January 26-27 (January 30-31)
Makhir 30 - Feast of Filling the Sacred Eye	January 13	January 29 (February 2)

Ancient Holiday	Kemetic Reform Date	Kemetic Orthodox (Reconstructionist)
Pa'en-Amunhotepu 1 - Feasts of Neith, Wadjit; Ptah Lifts the Sky in Esna	January 14	January 30 (February 3)
Pa'en-Amunhotepu 5 - Neith of Sais Goes Forth at Night	January 18	February 3 (February 7)
Pa'en-Amunhotepu 6 - Anubis Goes Forth With His Adorers	January 19	February 3 (February 8)
Pa'en-Amunhotepu 8 - The Gods Make Way for Khnum	January 20	February 6 (February 10)
Pa'en-Amunhotepu 9 - Fourth Feast of Wadjit	January 22	February 7 (February 11)
Pa'en-Amunhotepu 13 - Djehuty Goes Forth	January 26	February 16 (February 20)
Pa'en-Amunhotepu 18 - Feast of Nut	January 31	February 21 (February 25)

Ancient Holiday	Kemetic Reform Date	Kemetic Orthodox (Reconstructionist)
Pa'en-Amunhotepu 23 - Feast of Horus in Kem-Ur	February 5	February 21 (February 25)
Pa'en-Amunhotepu 28 - Feast of Osiris in Abydos, Raising the *trt* tree	February 10	February 26 (March 2)
Pa'en-Amunhotepu 29 - Amun Enters the Sky	February 11	February 27 (March 3)
Pa'en-Rennutet 1 - Wadjit Enters the Sky; Feasts of Neith, Khnum, Ra and His Eye	February 13	March 1 (March 5)
Pa'en-Rennutet 2 - Geb Goes Forth to Visit Anubis	February 14	March 2 (March 6)
Pa'en-Rennutet 4 - Min Goes to His Festival Tent; Feasts of Pakhet, Horus, Chewing Onions for Bastet	February 16	March 4 (March 8)

Ancient Holiday	Kemetic Reform Date	Kemetic Orthodox (Reconstructionist)
Pa'en-Rennutet 5 - Feast of Bastet in Her Barque	February 17	March 5 (March 9)
Pa'en-Rennutet 8 - Completing the Udjat-Eye of Horus	February 20	March 8 (March 12)
Pa'en-Rennutet 11 - Going Forth of Neith and Heka Child of Sais	February 23	March 11 (March 15)
Pa'en-Rennutet 16 - Khopri Goes Forth	February 28	March 16 (March 20)
Pa'en-Rennutet 19 - Ra Sails Forth in Iunu (Heliopolis)	March 3	March 19 (March 23)
Pa'en-Rennutet 20 - Appearing of Sobek in Ombos	March 4	March 20 (March 24)
Pa'en-Rennutet 28 - Feast of Horus-of-Sepa, Son of Sakhmet	March 12	March 28 (April 1)

Ancient Holiday	Kemetic Reform Date	Kemetic Orthodox (Reconstructionist)
Pa-Khonsu 1 - Feasts of Horus Son-of-Isis, Horus Sema-Tawy, Rennutet, Hathor *Iusa'as*; Amun-Min Goes Forth	March 15	March 31 (April 4)
Pa-Khonsu 4 - Chewing Onions for Bastet in Djeme	March 18	April 3 (April 7)
Pa-Khonsu 10 - Robing Anubis (*Dua* Anubis)	March 24	April 9 (April 13)
Pa-Khonsu 11 - Min Goes Forth in Djeme; Hathor Gives Birth	March 25	April 10 (April 14)
Pa-Khonsu 15 - Amun-Min Appears in Esna	March 29	April 14 (April 18)
Pa-Khonsu 19 - Going Forth of Khonsu	April 2	April 18 (April 22)

Ancient Holiday	Kemetic Reform Date	Kemetic Orthodox (Reconstructionist)
Pa-Khonsu 21 (approximate) - Birth of Horus, Son of Isis in Edfu	April 4	April 20 (April 24)
Pa-Khonsu 30 - Feasts of Min, Khonsu, Rennutet	April 13	April 29 (May 3)
Pa'en-Inet 1 - Khnum and Neith Go Forth at Esna; Feast of Hathor, Eye of Ra in Bubastis	April 14	April 30 (May 4)
Pa'en-Inet 1-2 (approximate) - Beautiful Feast of the Valley	April 14-15	April 30 - May 1 (May 4-5)
Pa'en-Inet 16 - Feast of Bastet, Purifying Sakhmet in Esna	April 29	May 15 (May 19)
Pa'en-Inet 26 - Revealing the Face in the House of Neith in Esna	May 9	May 25 (May 29)

Ancient Holiday	Kemetic Reform Date	Kemetic O... (Reconstru...)
Pa'en-Inet 30 - Shu Goes Forth to Bring Back Tefnut; Appearance of Djehuty; Appeasing Sakhmet in Esna	May 13	May 29 (June 2)
Apip 1 - Feast of Ipet-Hemet (Tawret)	May 14	May 30 (June 3)
Apip 7-17 (approximate) - Feast of the Beautiful Reunion	May 20-30	June 5-15 (June 9-19)
Apip 13 - Feast of Neith Who Saved Ra	May 26	June 11 (June 15)
Apip 14 - Eating Cucumbers by the Eye of Horus ("Cucumbers for Sakhmet")	May 27	June 12 (June 16)
Apip 19-20 – Appearance of Khnum, Grasping the Crook	June 1-2	June 17-18 (June 21-22)

Ancient Holiday	Kemetic Reform Date	Kemetic Orthodox (Reconstructionist)
Apip 29 - Feast of Mut of Isheru	June 11	June 27 (July 1)
Apip 30 - Feast of Apip	June 12	June 28 (July 2)
Mosu-Ra 1 - Feasts of Unnofer, Khnum-Ra; Going Forth of Hathor of Denderah and Her Ennead	June 13	June 29 (July 3)
Mosu-Ra 2 - Isis Luminous (Going Forth of Isis the Brilliant)	June 14	June 30 (July 4)
Mosu-Ra 3 - Her Majesty (Hathor) Goes Forth to Ra in Iunu	June 15	July 1 (July 5)
Mosu-Ra 4 - Feast of Seth	June 16	July 2 (July 6)
Mosu-Ra 5 - Min is at Akhmim	June 17	July 3 (July 7)

Ancient Holiday	Kemetic Reform Date	Kemetic Orthodox (Reconstructionist)
Mosu-Ra 22 - Feast of Anubis Upon-His-Mountain	July 4	July 20 (July 24)
Mosu-Ra 27 - Going Forth of Hathor	July 9	July 25 (July 29)
Mosu-Ra 28 - Feast of Min	July 10	July 26 (July 30)
Mosu-Ra 29 - Feast of Sokar in the House of Ptah	July 11	July 27 (July 31)
Mosu-Ra 30 - Day of Mosyt; Last Day of the Year	July 12	July 28 (August 1)
Heriu Diu Hir Ronpet:		
Birth of Osiris	July 13	July 29 (Aug. 2)
Birth of Horus	July 14	July 30 (Aug. 3)
Birth of Seth	July 15	July 31 (Aug. 4)
Birth of Isis	July 16	August 1 (Aug. 5)
Birth of Nephthys	July 17	August 2 (Aug. 6)

Special Readings For Feast Days

The following selections from historical liturgies are meant for major holidays and festival themes, including New Year's; the Opet Festival; the Osiris Mysteries and Raising of the *Djed*-pillar; the birth of Horus, and the Beautiful Feast of the Valley. Our first selection, the "Book of Knowing the Creations of Ra", is essentially the same text that was translated in prose form from the Papyrus Bremner-Rhind. That prose version is given in *Circle of the Sun* for the New Year's ritual of Overthrowing ~~Apophis~~. But it proved too difficult for some participants to read aloud in a dense paragraph. This lyric form proved much easier to follow, and has become part of our ongoing New Year's liturgy.

Book Of Knowing The Creations Of Ra

Thus Said The Lord Of All:

When I came into being,
Existence came into being.
I came into being as Khopri,
Came to be at the First Time;
I came to be as Khopri, and
Existence came into being.
I am older than the oldest,
Most primeval of all I have made;
For it is I who made the primeval time
And who made the primeval ones.
Many are those I created
Who came forth from my mouth
Before heaven existed,
Before earth existed,
Nor worms nor snakes
Existed in this place.
I made these inert ones in nun,
Where I had no place to stand.

I reflected in my heart,
I planned within my mind,
And I alone made all forms,
Before I had breathed out Shu
And before I spat out Tefnut,
Before any had come into being
Who could act with me.
I planned in my own heart,
There came to be many beings,
Forms of children and their children.
Then I lusted with my fist,
I made love with my hand
And spat with my own mouth.
I sneezed out Shu, I spat out Tefnut.
My father nun brought them up,
And I sent my eye for them
When they went far from me.
I had come into being alone,
But now there were three with me.
I came to be in this land
While Shu and Tefnut rejoiced in nun.
Whey brought me back my eye,
That I could unite my members,
And I wept over them.
That is how mankind came to be,
From the tears that flowed from my eye.
But then my eye raged at me,
For she found herself replaced,
The brilliant one in her stead.
So I placed her upon my brow
That she could rule all lands.
Thus did her wrath fall away,
For I replaced what was lost.
Then did Shu and Tefnut
beget Geb and Nut,

        then did Geb and Nut
     beget Osiris, Horus the eyeless,
        Seth, Isis and Nebet-hat,
     One after another from the womb,
  And they begat the multitudes of this land.
        They cast magic in my name
          To defeat my wicked foes;
        They cast magic in my name
         To fell the wicked A'apep.
     Oh you tears who fell from my eye,
  Oh you nine gods who came from my body,
        Be vigilant against Apophis!
        Chastise him in every place
           For the evil he has done!

Opet Hymn To Amun

(*from the Opet reliefs at Karnak, in* The Life of Meresamun)

Hail, oh Amun-Ra,
Lord of thrones of the two lands,
May you live forever!
A drinking place is hewn out,
The sky folded back to the south.
A drinking place is hewn out,
The sky folded back to the north.

Hail, oh Amun-Ra,
First one of the two lands,
Foremost one in Karnak,
In splendid appearance in your fleet,
In your beautiful feast of Opet,
May you be pleased with it!
A drinking place is built
For you in the ship of ships.
The paths of the twin horizons
Have been bound up for you;
A great flood has been raised up.
May you pacify the Two Ladies,
Oh Lord of the Red and White crowns,
Oh Horus strong of arm!

Litany to Ma'at and Ra

(from the late 18th dynasty tomb of Nefer-hotep)

Oh Ra who sets with Ma'at,
Ma'at is joined to his brow.
Oh Ra who rises with Ma'at,
Ma'at embraces his beauty.
Oh Ra, effective through Ma'at,
Ma'at is secured to his bark.
Oh Ra mighty through Ma'at,
whereon he lives every day.
Oh Ra who made Ma'at,
and whom one offers Ma'at:
You placed Ma'at in my heart
that I may raise her up to your ka!
I know you live by her
and it is you who made her body.
I am a straight one free of lies,
who does not practice deception.

From The Lamentations Of Isis And Nephthys

Isis speaks:
Come to your house, come to your house!
You of Iunu, come to your house,
Your foes are no more!

Oh good husband, come to your house!
Behold me, I am your beloved sister,
You shall not part from me!

(***Isis continued:***)

Oh good youth, come to your house!
Long, long have I not seen you!
My heart mourns for you, my eyes seek you,
How I search to see you!

Shall I not see you, shall I not see you,
Good king, shall I not see you?

I am your sister, your wife,
You shall not leave me!
Gods and men look for you,
Weeping for you together!

Nephthys speaks:
Oh good king, come to your house!
Please your heart, your foes are all gone!
Your two sisters beside you guard your tomb,
Calling for you in tears!

Turn around in your tomb!
See us women, speak to us!
Oh king, drive all pain from our hearts!

Your court of gods and men beholds you,
Show them your face, great lord!
Let your face not shun our faces,
For our hearts are glad to see you!

I am Nephthys, your beloved sister!
Your foe is fallen, he shall not be!
I am with you, your bodyguard,
For all eternity!

(*continued next page*)

Isis speaks:
Your sacred image, Orion in heaven,
Rises and sets every day;
I am Sothis who follows him,
I will not depart from him!

The sky has your soul, the earth your body,
The netherworld is filled with your secrets.
Your wife is your guard,
While your son Horus rules your lands!

Nephthys speaks:
The souls of your forefathers are your companions,
Your son Horus, child of Isis, is before you;
I am the light that guards you every day,
I shall not leave you ever!

Isis speaks:
Your court of gods and men,
With Horus, perform your rites;
Come to your followers, Osiris, lord,
Do not part from them!

Hymn For Raising The Djed:

*(adapted from the Dramatic Ramesseum papyrus
and the tomb of Kheru-ef)*

Sistrums for your ka and *menat* for your gracious face as you arise,
Oh august *Djed*, Osiris-Sokar, lord of Shetyt!

Osir-Sokar appears in glory;
Praised are you now!
Exalted are you, o rudder;
You join with the land
That you may travel it.
May Ra favor you for your goodness.
Come, let us exalt him!

You have filled the Two Lands with your beauty,
Radiant and reborn as the sun in the sky.

The Birth Of Horus

(adapted from Coffin Text 148)

Speaking roles: Atum, Isis, Horus, narration (optional)

Narration/Atum:
Lightning flashes, the gods are afraid,
Isis wakes pregnant with the seed of Osiris.
She is uplifted, her heart is glad.

Isis:
"Oh you gods! I am Isis,
Sister of Osiris,
Who wept for the lord of the Two Lands!

His seed is in my womb,
A God within the egg,
Foremost of the Ennead!

He shall rule over this land,
He shall avenge his father,
He shall slay the murderer.

Come, oh you Gods, protect him,
For you know him in your hearts!"

Atum:
"Guard your heart, oh woman!" so says Atum.

Isis:
"He takes shape even now," says Isis,
"This god in the egg, heir to the Ennead;
I am Isis, most august of the Gods,
This god in my womb is the seed of Osiris!"

Atum:
Thus says Atum,
"Keep hidden, oh Isis!
Indeed you shall give birth
To the heir of Osiris.
May his father's killer
Not find him, not harm him!"

Isis:
"Hear these words, oh you Gods!
Our protection decreed
By Atum, lord of all!
Servants of your father
Shall serve you, oh Horus,
Come forth upon the earth!"

Horus:

"I am Horus, oh you Gods!
I am Horus, the falcon!
I fly to the horizon
Pass over those in the sky!
My foe shall never reach me,
For my place is far from Seth,
Enemy of my father!

I fly forth into the dawn,
No god can do what I do.
I shall prevail against my foe,
Set him under my sandals.
I am Horus, more lofty
Than men or than the gods;
I am Horus, son of Isis!"

Feast of the Valley Hymn:

O Amun, heaven is uplifted for You,
Ground is trodden for You.
Ptah with His two hands makes a chapel
As a resting place for Your heart.

How great is Amun, beloved god!
He rises in Karnak, His city, Lord of Life!
The beautiful face of Amun, beloved power,
Whom the gods love to behold,
Mighty One who came from the horizon!
All of Amun's domain is in feast.
Happy it is for Amun-Ra,
The One whom mankind adores!

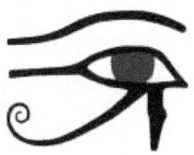

Online Resources

In the heady days of the early Internet, Kemetic resources - and thus options - were extremely limited. Now, the opposite is true; a beginner can easily get swept up in a current of social media groups, blogs, forums, web pages, and-and-and...! This list of suggested sources is necessarily limited, but consists of communities and sources containing beginner-friendly but still knowledgeable and reliable people and information.

Kemetic Independent Channel:
http://www.youtube.com/user/KemeticIndependent
Chances are high that you found this book through the YouTube channel - but if not, log in and subscribe! You can not only watch hours of content on Kemetic and Egyptian Pagan practice, but also ask questions that could become topics in future episodes.

Kemetic Reform Online:
www.kemeticreform.org
Home page for the nascent Kemetic Reform tradition. Many of the other resources listed here can be found on the Kemetic Reform site as well. As our tradition develops, more information and resources will be uploaded, so add this site to your favorites and check back every so often!

Following the Sun discussion forum:
http://followingthesun.freeforums.org/
Our forum's home site since 2010, Freeforums, was recently purchased by Tapatalk and has recently undergone some cosmetic changes as a result. But you can still join the discussion with fellow Kemetics and Egyptian Pagans of various traditions.

Henadology Blog's Egyptian A-Z:
http://henadology.wordpress.com/theology/netjeru/
This is positively one of the best-researched blogs on Egyptian deities online, and comes highly recommended. If you were looking for a deity that was not in this book, the Henadology Blog probably has Them. What's even better, all of the sources cited are historical, academically-sound material; no 'conspiracy theories' or unverified gnoses to be found here.

Online Academic Research:

Oriental Institute of the University of Chicago:
https://oi.uchicago.edu/research
The University of Chicago's Oriental Institute hosts one of the most prestigious Egyptology programs in the United States, and publishes the Journal of Near Eastern Studies (JNES). By clicking on the "Publications" link, you can find several of the sources I cite in my bibliography, plus many more, downloadable as .PDF files. Have fun!

Digital Egypt for Universities:
http://www.ucl.ac.uk/museums-static/digitalegypt//Welcome.html

University College London's Petrie Museum and Egyptology Department, another prestigious program based in the UK, maintains this website. Select the 'A-Z Index' at the top and pick your topics from there; they have an extensive list of translated spells from the Book of the Dead, among other interesting topics.

Osirisnet.net:
https://osirisnet.net/e_centrale.htm

This is the English-language version of a website is maintained by French Egyptologists working in Egypt. Their photos and virtual tours are engrossing, and their articles can be helpful resources when looking for information on specific topics.

JStor:
https://www.jstor.org/jpass/

JStor is an online academic journal archive that includes important journals for ancient Egyptian studies, such as the Journal of Egyptian Archaeology (JEA), Journal of Near Eastern Studies (JNES), and Journal of the American Research Center in Egypt (JARCE). **Take note:** *Access to JStor is not free* **unless** *you use a public or university library. But the link above gives options for subscription plans, if you wish to conduct private research outside of a library system.*

Academia.edu:
https://www.academia.edu/

A free resource for recently published papers, Academia.edu operates like a cross between a social media platform - you can even log in with Facebook or Google, though if you're concerned about privacy I recommend creating your own account - and a traditional academic network. You can even sign up to get email updates on topics relevant to your topics of interest.

Bibliography

Adler, Margot. Drawing Down the Moon: Witches, Druids, Goddess-Worshippers and Other Pagans in America. New York: Penguin Press, 2006.

Allen, George T. "Some Egyptian Sun Hymns". *Journal of Near Eastern Archaeology,* vol. 8, no. 4, 1949, pp. 349-355.

Allen, James P. The Ancient Egyptian Pyramid Texts. Society of Biblical Literature, 2005.

Assman, Jan. The Search for God in Ancient Egypt. Translated by David Lorton, Cornell University Press, 2001.

Barbash, Yekaterina. Divine Felines: Cats of Ancient Egypt. New York: Brooklyn Museum, 2016.

Betz, Hans Dieter, ed. The Greek Magical Papyri in Translation, Second Edition. University of Chicago Press, 1996.

Budge, E. A. Wallis. The Egyptian Book of the Dead. New York: Dover Publications, 1967.

--------------------------. The Gods of the Egyptians, vols. I-II, 1909. New York: Dover Publications, 1969.

Cauville, Sylvie. Offerings to the Gods in Egyptian Temples. Translated by Bram Calcoen, Leuven, Paris, Walpole: Peeters, 2012.

Darnell, John Coleman. "The Apotropaic Goddess in the Eye". *Studien zur Altägytischen Kultur,* Bd. 24, 1997. pp. 35-48.

----------------------------. "Hathor Returns to Medamud". *Studien zur Altägytischen Kultur*, Bd. 22, 1995. pp. 47-94.

El-Sabban, Sherif. The Temple Calendars of Ancient Egypt. 1992. University of Liverpool, PhD dissertation.

El-Sayed, Ramadan. La Déesse Neith de Sais, vol. I: Importance et Rayonnement de Son Culte. Cairo: Institute Français D'Archéologie Orientale, 1982.

Faulkner, Raymond O. Ancient Egyptian Book of the Dead. New York: Fall River Press, 2010.

----------------------------. The Ancient Egyptian Coffin Texts. Oxford: Aris and Phillips, 2007.

----------------------------. "The Bremner-Rhind Papyrus - II". *Journal of Egyptian Archaeology*, vol. 23, no. 1, 1937, pp. 10-16.

----------------------------. "The Bremner-Rhind Papyrus III: The Book of Overthrowing 'Apep". *Journal of Egyptian Archaeology*, vol. 23, no. 2, 1937, pp. 166-185.

----------------------------. "The Bremner-Rhind Papyrus: IV". *Journal of Egyptian Archaeology*, vol. 24, no. 1, 1938, pp. 41-53.

Finnestad, Ragnhild Bjerre. Image of the World and Symbol of the Creator: On the Cosmological and Iconological Values of the Temple of Edfu. *Studies in Oriental Religions*, vol. 10, 1985.

Fisher, Marjorie M., Lacovera, Peter, et al. Ancient Nubia: African Kingdoms on the Nile. New York, Cairo: American University in Cairo Press, 2012.

Frankfurter, David. Religion in Roman Egypt: Assimilation and Resistance. Princeton University Press, 1998.

Frood, Elizabeth. Biographical Texts From Ramessid Egypt. Society of Biblical Literature, 2007, pp. 119, 121, 168, 174. *Google Books*, Web. 1 July 2018.

Gillam, Robyn. Performance and Drama in Ancient Egypt. London: Duckworth and Co., 2005.

Hawass, Zahi. "Foreword", Anubis, Upwawet and Other Deities: Personal Worship and Official Religion in Ancient Egypt. American University in Cairo Press, 2007, 1. *Google Books*, Web. 1 July 2018.

Kemp, Barry. How to Read the Egyptian Book of the Dead. W.W. Norton and Company, 2007, pp. 17-22.

King, Karen L., et al. Women and Goddess Traditions: in Antiquity and Today. Minneapolis: Fortress Press, 1997.

Klotz, David. "Adoration of the Ram: Five Hymns to Amun-Re from Hibis Temple." *Yale Egyptological Studies 6.* New Haven: Yale Egyptological Seminar, 2006.

----------------. "The Theban Cult of Chonsu the Child in the Ptolemaic Period." *Documents de Théologies Thébaines Tardives* 1, *CENiM* 3, Montepellier, 2009, pp. 95-134.

Kockelmann, Holger. "A Roman Period Demotic Manual of Hymns to Rattawy and Other Deities (P. Ashm. 1984.76)". *Journal of Egyptian Archaeology*, vol. 89, 2003, pp. 217-229.

Kozloff, Arielle P. "Ritual Implements and Related Statuettes". In Egypt's Dazzling Sun: Amenhotep III and His World, Kozloff,

Bryan, et al, editors. Cleveland Museum of Art, 1992, p. 337

Lesko, Barbara. The Great Goddesses of Egypt. Norman: University of Oklahoma Press, 1999.

Lichtheim, Miriam. Ancient Egyptian Literature, vols. I-III. Berkeley: University of California Press, 1973, 1980, 2006.

McDonald, Kathleen. How to Meditate: A Practical Guide. Boston: Wisdom Publications, 2005.

Millard, Dom Bede. "St. Christopher and the Lunar Disc of Anubis". *Journal of Egyptian Archaeology*, vol. 73, 1987, pp. 237-238.

Murnane, William J. "United With Eternity: A Concise Guide to the Monuments of Medinet Habu." Oriental Institute: Egyptian Civilization. 1980. Oriental Institute of the University of Chicago. Accessed 23 January 2012.
http://oi.uchicago.edu/research/pubs/catalog/misc/united.html

Nelson, Harold H. "Certain Reliefs at Karnak and Medinet Habu and the Ritual of Amenophis I." *Journal of Near Eastern Studies*, vol. 8, no. 3, 1949. pp. 201-232.

----------------------. "Certain Reliefs at Karnak and Medinet Habu and the Ritual of Amenophis I-(Concluded)." *Journal of Near Eastern Studies*, vol. 8, no. 4, 1949. pp. 310-345.

Parker, Richard A. "The Calendars of Ancient Egypt." Oriental Institute: Egyptian Civilization. 1950. Oriental Institute of the University of Chicago. Accessed 4 November 2010.
https://oi.uchicago.edu/research/pubs/catalog/saoc/saoc26.html

Pinch, Geraldine. Egyptian Mythology: A Guide to the Gods, Goddesses and Traditions of Ancient Egypt. Oxford University Press, 2002.

Quirke, Stephen. The Cult of Ra: Sun-Worship in Ancient Egypt. Thames and Hudson, 2001.

Quirke, Stephen, et al. "Festival Dates in the Ancient Egyptian Calendar." *Digital Egypt for Universities.* University College London, 2003. Accessed March 2013. http://www.ucl.ac.uk/museums-static/digitalegypt//ideology/festivaldates.html

----------------------------. "A late Middle Kingdom account, listing festivals." *Digital Egypt for Universities.* University College London, 2003. Accessed March 2013. http://www.ucl.ac.uk/museums-static/digitalegypt//lahun/festivallistmk.html

Reed, Ellen Cannon. Circle of Isis: Ancient Egyptian Magic for Modern Witches. Franklin Lakes: New Page Books, 2002.

Ritner, Robert K. "O. Gardiner 363: A Spell Against Night Terrors". *Journal of the American Research Center in Egypt*, vol. 27, 1990. pp. 25-41.

Rosenow, Daniela. "The Naos of 'Bastet, Lady of the Shrine' from Bubastis." *Journal of Egyptian Archaeology*, vol. 94, 2008. pp. 247-266.

Sauneron, Serge. The Priests of Ancient Egypt. Translated by David Lorton. Cornell University Press, 2000.

Singer, Margaret Thaler. Cults in Our Midst: The Continuing Fight Against Their Hidden Menace. Revised Edition. Jossey-Bass, 2003. pp. 137-139.

Shaw, Ian, and Nicholson, Paul. The Dictionary of Ancient Egypt. New York: Harry N. Abrams, Inc., 1995.

Spalinger, Anthony. "The Festival Structure of Thutmose III's Buto Stele". *Journal of the American Research Center in Egypt*, vol. 33, 1996, pp. 69-76.

------------------------. "A Chronological Analysis of the Feast of thy". *Studien zur Altägytischen Kultur*, Bd. 20, 1993, pp. 289-303.

Stewart, H. M. "A Crossword Hymn to Mut". *Journal of Egyptian Archaeology,* vol. 57, 1971. pp. 87-104.

Szpakowska, Kasia. "Playing With Fire: Initial Observations on the Religious Uses of Clay Cobras from Amarna". *Journal of the American Research Center in Egypt*, vol. 40, 2003. pp. 113-122.

Teeter, Emily, and Johnson, Janet J. "The Life of Meresamun: A Temple Singer in Ancient Egypt." Oriental Institute: Egyptian Civilization. 2009. Oriental Institute of the University of Chicago. Accessed 15 October 2010. https://oi.uchicago.edu/research/pubs/catalog/oimp/oimp29.html

Zakbar, L. V. "Six Hymns to Isis in the Sanctuary of Her Temple at Philae and Their Theological Significance. Part I." *Journal of Egyptian Archaeology*, vol. 69, 1983. pp. 115-137.

CPSIA information can be obtained
at www.ICGtesting.com
Printed in the USA
LVHW091346120419
613978LV00001B/98/P